HOW TO REPAIR AND DRESS OLD DOLLS

WRITTEN AND ILLUSTRATED
BY AUDREY JOHNSON

CHARLES T. BRANFORD COMPANY
NEWTON MASSACHUSETTS 02159

York House, Portugal Street,
London, W.C. 2

U.S. Edition 1967

Library of Congress Catalog Card Number
67-12386

Reprinted 1969

ALSO BY AUDREY JOHNSON

How to Make Dolls' Houses

Audrey Johnson gives full instructions for building a variety of attractive houses which can be constructed by anyone reasonably good with their hands. They range from a model schoolhouse which children can make with inexpensive materials, a modern house and a shop, to a selection including a Westmorland Farmhouse, a Tall Villa and a Seaside Boarding House.

ART AND CRAFT EDUCATION: '. . . a delightfully unusual book which is a pleasure to read . . . fascinating variety of dolls' houses.'

Illustrated. $2.95 net

---

*Printed in Great Britain by
The Camelot Press Ltd., London and Southampton*

Contents

Introduction

MY FIRST INTEREST was for dolls' houses, which I made and sold, most unprofitably. This led to a book on how to make dolls' houses and inevitably to a wider acquaintance with the collectors of toys and dolls. I could never resist the slightly damaged doll that was going for a few shillings on a market stall, and friends who collected dolls would ask me to have a go at repairing their cracked dolls, knowing I was a painter and enjoyed working with my hands, and so I gradually acquired some skill and knowledge and even a modest collection of dolls. It appears to me that the acquisition of a large collection of dolls in mint condition requires little else but money and determination, whilst considerably more pleasure must be had by those who have slowly built up an enviable collection as a result of their patience and skill. Dolls, even modern ones, are fragile objects, exposed for their first few years to peculiarly harsh treatment, so that only a few must survive, and it is rather tragic if those with only minor wounds should be discarded with the rest. It is hardly necessary for me to attempt to justify or explain the passion for collecting.

A surprisingly large number of people find great pleasure in building up collections of dolls, and this interest has been reflected very noticeably in the museums. Long neglected cases of dolls and toys have suddenly been furbished up and brought to the fore and this has obviously created more interest and understanding. Dolls and toys, kept presumably for reasons of sentiment, have suddenly acquired a more material status when their twins have been seen in the showcases of museums.

When I first came to the problem of repairing such dolls, I had the advantages of a painter's training; some general knowledge of making moulds, dyeing cloth, embroidery and so on, and a reasonably informed eye for historical costume. I knew, at least, where to look for more detailed information and found, as ever, that there was a great deal more to be learnt than I had ever imagined possible.

I have not, as yet, encountered any book that deals exclusively with the problem of how to repair and re-dress old dolls, although information is scattered through books about dolls and toys, books primarily concerned with history and scholarship, and I have checked such information as far as I am able against my own practical experience.

This book is intended to be a 'how to do it' book, a primer for those who are interested in old dolls but without experience of their repair, and I hope that it may be of some use to those with far greater scholarship than I, who have collections in their care.

A less obvious, but perhaps wider, use for the book could be in schools where the dressing of dolls has been used to further the imaginative development of small children, whilst giving them some practical experience of sewing, together with a little historical sense.

The subject falls naturally enough into two major sections—the body with its head and limbs, and the clothing. The first section is therefore concerned primarily with techniques of repair and the second with matters of history, and for this I have attempted to provide a simple pictorial guide to the styles of costume most likely to be encountered, together with some specific examples from my own experience. There are, of course, books about dolls and books about historical costume and to these the would-be restorer will inevitably have recourse but, as he or she is unlikely to own many of them, I hope this little handbook may prove useful.

So that I might write from direct practical experience, rather than from memory or reference, I asked Miss Helena Gibson, the Director of the Harris Museum at Preston, to let me repair those dolls that were so damaged as to be unsuitable for display in their interesting collection. This has been a great help and has enabled me to use examples of dolls that would normally be too rare and valuable to come my way.

At the end of the book I have listed some collections of dolls, for it is only by a familiarity, gradually acquired, that the restorer can become confident of his ability to date, repair and reclothe.

I do not include a bibliography or refer to sources very often, as I would consider such practice beyond the scope of a book which sets out primarily to stimulate and to help those wishing to acquire skill and experience in a delicate but entertaining task.

American equivalents, or descriptions, of British proprietary products mentioned in this book are given on page 128.

SECTION 1

The Head

EVERY CONCEIVABLE MATERIAL has been used for making dolls' heads and the most successful and therefore the most often encountered are wood, wax, papier-mâché, composition, metal, rubber, celluloid, china, Parian, bisque and, of course, plastic.

Fig. 1

WOOD has been used from the earliest times and those few dolls that survive from before the 19th century are likely to be too delicate and are almost certainly too valuable to be restored by the amateur. I shall therefore begin with the so-called 'Dutch Dolls', carved and turned on lathes by the country people of Europe during the long winter evenings.

If the damage is only superficial—scratches and so on—then I would be reluctant to lose the attractive patina of age and would confine myself to a gentle cleaning, starting with the less important areas and using a mild soap and lukewarm water.

Occasionally, you will encounter woodworm, and the small holes should be individually injected with one of the patent insecticides such as 'Rentokil', and then filled with a specially prepared plaster such as 'Polyfilla'. The white dot that results from this can be disguised by painting it with tempera colours to match the rest of the surface.

If the head has been coated with gesso (a thin layer of plaster), which has cracked and largely fallen away, then it will all have to come off. The colouring that remains will then be lost, so it would be well, at this stage, to make sure that it will not be forgotten, either by making a drawing or writing a description of it, preferably both. The old gesso can then be rubbed away with fine worn sandpaper and several thin coats of new gesso applied.

Gesso can be bought at most shops that sell artists' materials. It is a smoothly ground plaster, needing only to be mixed with water to the consistency of cream before its application with a soft brush in several thin coats. Each coat is allowed to go hard enough for a rub down with fine sandpaper.

If only a small patch of the original gesso has fallen away, then obviously it would be more sensible to replace the missing section rather than the whole, using the same technique. This is a delicate task, but quite practicable.

Once the gesso is thoroughly hard, then the whole must be coloured and, if necessary, varnished to simulate the original. For this, I have found tempera colours the most efficient, for they dry quickly enough for successive coats to be applied within minutes and enable the final effect to be achieved gradually on the head itself. Such tempera colours are manufactured and sold in tubes by most artists' colourmen. I use Rowney's egg tempera colours and the plastic 'Cryla' colours. Both have water as a medium and give a mat finish that can be gently polished with silk. The 'Cryla' colours can be varnished fairly soon with their own special medium if a shiny effect is necessary. The egg tempera has to be allowed much longer to harden before a varnish can be applied.

To paint the flesh, I use white, black, cadmium red and yellow ochre in such combination as the subject demands. For the eyes I use ultramarine and for the eyebrows a variety of browns. Obviously some experience in mixing these colours is necessary and it is readily acquired with a little practice.

It is necessary always to keep in mind that the doll is old and that your painting should suggest a worn and darkened surface, not the fresh complexion of a living child.

Fig. 2. A wax head

WAX was used a great deal and for the most beautiful and elaborate dolls.

It was a modelling material for thousands of years and was certainly used for dolls in the latter half of the 16th century, and then extensively for dolls' heads in the 18th and 19th centuries, in Germany, France and England. It is an adaptable material, so there are three commonly used methods for making wax dolls' heads: solid, moulded and dipped.

The solid heads were either carved from the block or moulded by hand when the wax was heated to 95° F.

The moulded heads were made by melting the wax and pouring it into moulds to form several layers, each 3 or 4 millimetres thick.

The dipped heads are those where a coating of melted wax has been poured over some other material such as plaster, wood, metal, papier-mâché, or, more often, composition.

All wax heads are rather delicate, for they can be softened by exposure to excessive heat, whilst a strong light will cause their colouring to fade. Their restoration is a difficult and delicate operation and it is often advisable to leave well alone, even when the head is badly damaged—confining yourself to a rearrangement of hair to cover the top half and a high-necked collar for the throat. Superficial dirt can be gently removed with face cream and a soft cloth. Sometimes a patina of yellow dirt has collected in the hollows on the doll's face and this has hardened too much to be removed with face cream; this can be gently rubbed with genuine turpentine on a soft cloth. Turpentine does, in fact, dissolve the wax very slightly, so this has to be carefully handled; and it will, of course, remove the colour that has been applied to the cheeks and this will need repainting.

Slight cracks can also be repaired with this method; if necessary, warm the turpentine rag and this will spread the wax into the cracks. Although cracks are the most common faults with wax dolls, each needs different treatment for, in some cases, the wax is thick on the head and others have a much thinner layer. These are the easiest to repair and another method of restoration that I have used for these is to soak a piece of cotton wool in very hot water and rub this over the crack until the wax is soft enough to spread. If the crack is black with dirt, a little soap on the cotton wool cleans it at the same time.

A much loved, indeed over loved, wax doll has often been used so much that the nose has almost worn away and I have found that the simplest way to restore this feature is to get your hands very hot and, in a very warm atmosphere, coax the wax surrounding the nose towards the centre until a new nose can make at least a vestigial appearance.

When the surface of the wax has been finely cracked with age, but not too pulled asunder, then it is often possible to fill these small fissures by using a warm needle and spreading the surface wax into the gaps.

When the cracks are too big for this method to work, then a little wax may be stolen from another part of the head, where the loss can be hidden by clothes or hair, and this bit of wax may be rolled between hot fingers until it can be pressed gently into the crack. Incidentally, you must be careful to clear away any dirt from old cracks or their filling will show as a dark and grubby line.

A spoon handle warmed in a pan of hot water will help to smooth off the surface, but rarely, if ever, will this method of repair render the damage wholly invisible. Nevertheless, it will make an old doll look a lot better, and it is, I believe, preferable to more drastic work that is likely to leave you with all too new a doll's head.

Many early moulded wax dolls had a slit in the top of the head into which the hair had been pushed. The wax had then been softened and pressed on to the hair to fix it into position. With time and use, this slit would inevitably reopen and extend down the face, and this common fault may be remedied by the methods that I have just described.

Should you acquire a dipped wax doll that has been so badly damaged that it is beyond these methods of restoration, then it is often possible to give it a new layer of wax.

Separate the head from the body and from the hair so that you can handle it freely, and break away the fragments of wax with your fingernail or with a nail-file. The support can then be recoloured or touched up with tempera colours, for they will show through the wafer-thin layer of wax that you are later to apply.

There is never enough of the old wax just simply to melt and put back, so a new lot of wax must be made.

Beeswax is the commonest type in use, but it is rather sticky and difficult to handle. Melted candles are more transparent and harder and therefore very suitable for a thin coat, whilst the beeswax looks better if you have a thick layer. A mixture of the two seems to make a reasonable compromise. This creamy-coloured wax can be tinted by mixing in bits of coloured candle or wax crayon, or lipstick although whether you do this or not will depend on what you are trying to replace or imitate.

The wax should be melted in a vessel large enough for you to dip the whole head. You can try it out for colour by dipping strips of card that match the colour of the head, for it sets very quickly. When you are confident that you have the correct colour of wax ready, slip your hand or fingers into the shoulders of the doll's head and dip it in and out of the wax very quickly. The hotter the wax, the thinner the coat. I have found that as soon as the wax has melted over a very slow heat then it is just about right for dipping—but it is as well to experiment for yourself. Should you wish to start again, then you can remove almost all the wax by dipping it into *very* hot wax, but you must let everything cool down before you start again from the beginning.

Having achieved a satisfactory coat of wax, you may then take a fine sharp blade, such as a balsa wood knife, and cut away the wax from over the eyes. If you do this while it is still warm it should come away quite neatly and leave the eyes bright and clear.

Once the layer of wax has thoroughly hardened, the features may be painted—eyebrows, lashes, lips and cheeks—and for this I have found oil colours to be the most suitable, for they are transparent and do not spoil the glow and feeling of depth that is so characteristic of the wax doll's head. These features must be drawn on very delicately indeed, and the cheeks are best coloured by rubbing the paint on with a finger-tip rather than a brush.

Finally, may I say again that wax dolls' heads are hard to repair, and it is heartbreaking to lose all because of a single slip. Better to use camouflage than attempt too bold a restoration; and it is certainly essential to become familiar with the use of molten wax.

PAPIER-MÂCHÉ and *COMPOSITION* are very similar tough materials made either from pulped paper, water, size, paste and whiting or from sheets of paper glued together, or from similar patent mixtures. I describe how to make papier-mâché in a later chapter dealing with the *BODY* (pages 49–51).

Papier-mâché can be modelled or moulded and, when dry, it can be sandpapered smooth and painted. A strong, resilient material, it is ideal for dolls' heads and is used either as a base for wax or as a material in its own right. As far as is known, it was first used for dolls in Germany in about 1810 and it was certainly in use in France and Italy early in the 19th century.

Composition is very similar and is used in the same way, but it is a mixture of many things, such as plaster of paris, bran, sawdust and glue. It has been widely used for heads, bodies and limbs since the early 19th century, and by 1844 we find dolls with composition heads inset with glass eyes and glass teeth.

To clean heads made from these materials, you can wipe them gently with a little grease solvent or with soapy water that has had a little ammonia added to it. It is as well to try out such solvents on a hidden portion, such as the shoulders, and if the colouring comes away then it is probably safest to confine yourself to cleaning it with breadcrumbs. Dents and cracks can be filled with Polyfilla or plastic wood, which has to be allowed to harden before it can be sandpapered flush with the adjoining surface.

The colouring can now be matched with artists' tempera colours in the same manner as for wooden heads.

It is essential to try out the colours on a bit of card or some hidden portion of the head, for the original colouring of the head will usually be found to be much darker than appeared likely, so that you will have to apply a particularly grubby-looking mixture to make a flesh colour.

METAL was occasionally used for dolls' heads, and you may encounter brass ones that were made in Germany, or tin ones made there during and after the First World War. They were coloured with a bright enamel paint, so naturally enough they can be restored with similar enamels that can be bought in little tins almost anywhere.

RUBBER dolls were made from 1840 onwards, the indiarubber being cast in metal moulds.

Unfortunately, such a flexible support allowed the skin of paint to crack very readily, and whatever remains must first be removed before repainting. They can be rubbed smooth and clean with a scrap of old worn sandpaper and then repainted with oil colours. Again, you must remember to record what evidence remains of the old features before obliterating them.

CELLULOID was a highly inflammable and, for children's toys, a particularly dangerous material, but it was used for dolls from about 1880 onwards.

It is a hard plastic compound made by subjecting guncotton,

camphor and other materials to hydraulic pressure. Celluloid dents very easily and this is the commonest fault. The dents can sometimes be removed by holding the affected part in very

Fig. 3. A celluloid head

hot water to soften it a little and then pressing round the edges of the dent in the hope that the centre may spring forward. If you can get at it from the back or inside, so much the better; but, if not, then you can try puncturing the dent with a fine needle and pulling forward.

The colouring is an integral part of the material, but it fades and leaves a very jaundiced complexion that can be rejuvenated with oil colours. Again the pink is best applied to cheeks with the finger-tips in the same manner as rouge was once applied to human cheeks.

To avoid losing all evidence of the celluloid texture it is as well to retouch the complexion rather than repaint with an even coat.

Fig. 4. A plastic head

PLASTIC, as we understand the term, has been used for dolls since the Second World War and it can vary a great deal in its effect. Plastic will often imitate the texture of human flesh so well that it may be considered unpleasant. It will usually clean with a grease solvent. Some less-efficient plastics may nevertheless fade and can only be restored with paint made from the same or similar material. A great many household paints are made from plastic and, if they are, it will say so on the tin. The fairly recently introduced artists' Cryla colours are plastic and suitable for this purpose, although I would again advise retouching only the essential parts, to give a healthier appearance, and of course the repainting of lips and eyes if this is necessary.

Should the moulded seams of these dolls have opened, as they frequently do, then they can best be rejoined by the application of a hot knitting-needle, which should make the plastic edges sticky enough to join when held quickly and firmly together.

A less dashing, but safer, way is to hold the split over a steaming kettle until it is softened and then push together and hold until it is cold and hard.

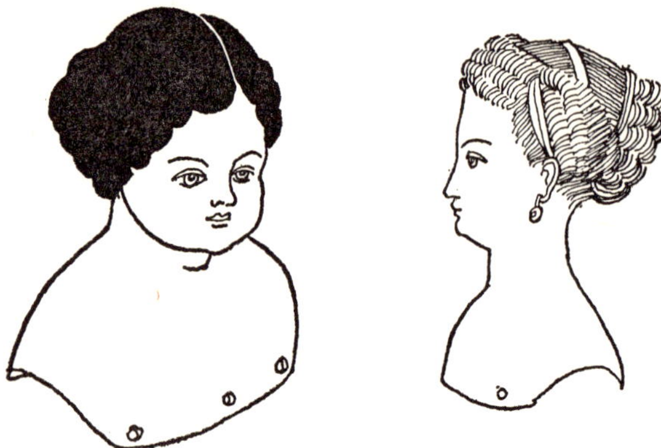

Figs. 5 and 6. Ceramic heads

CERAMIC dolls' heads are of three kinds, China, Parian and Bisque, although the term China is often used to describe any such doll.

China heads are those of highly glazed white porcelain with the black hair painted on top, so popular in the 19th century.

The Parian heads are made from a very fine, high-fired white clay, but they are unglazed and give the effect of marble, for the material originally set out to imitate the marble from the Greek island of Paros. They are usually blonde because, I understand, the manufacturers considered fair hair a better match for Parian ware.

A greater number and variety of dolls have been made from Bisque, which is again unglazed clay, with the colour painted on to the clay and fired to give the flesh tints.

It is not my intention to write at greater length about these materials except where it directly concerns repair and redecoration.

A lot of badly cracked dolls can be successfully camouflaged by using new hairstyles, or with a necklace or high-necked dress.

Fig. 7. A bisque head

The bisque dolls are, of course, slightly absorbent and may have old dirt and grease soaked into their pores. This should wash off with a little ammonia in warm, soapy water, but if obstinate black marks remain then a mild abrasive (such as is sold for cleaning baths) can be tried—but gently.

All too often a broken head has been badly repaired a long time ago and when this is the case it is necessary to soak the glue away from the joins and start afresh so that you can take advantage of the more efficient and less obtrusive glues that are now available.

The clear glues that evaporate quickly, and usually smell of pear drops, make the least visible joins, and it is best to do one piece at a time and to have sufficient patience to allow them to set firmly before going on to the next. Hold the pieces into position with rubber bands and start repairing at the front so that you finish at the back where it is less likely to show. Excess glue may be removed with a solvent or a razor blade.

If small fragments are missing, then a piece of cloth should be glued across the back of the damaged area to form a support that can later be filled with fine plaster, which will finally be coloured to match the rest of the head or, in the case of Parian dolls, left white. Dental plaster is the finest for this purpose and can be bought at most chemists' shops (Polyfilla will do for this job, but it is rather coarser.) The plaster can be tinted by mixing water colours with the water when you mix it, but if the result still doesn't match the head, then you can use the water colours, mixed with white, to touch up; but this only after it has hardened and been rubbed down carefully with the finest of sandpapers.

To imitate the texture of bisque, you can finish off with a very light wax polish.

To hide small cracks—wash them first with a very strong solution of bleach, applied with a feather, and then push in plaster of paris or the white glue known as Copydex. Wiped thoroughly clean, this disguises the cracks very well.

The highly glazed china dolls can be repaired in the same way, but the filling will have to be painted with enamel colours, as with metal dolls, and several coats may be necessary to get the desired effect.

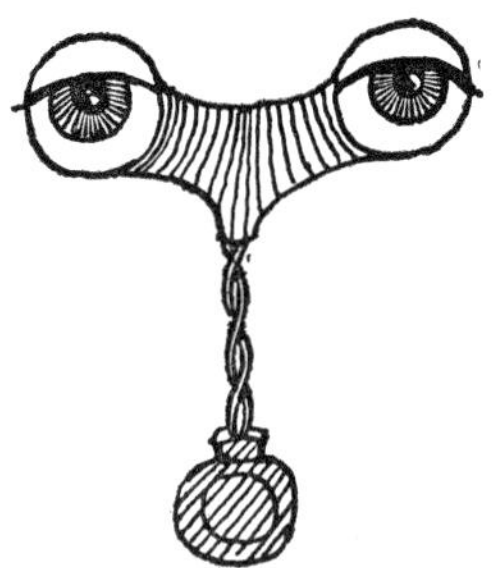

The Eyes

From the earliest times the eyes have been either painted directly on to the face or made of glass.

Occasionally, and most often with home-made dolls, other things have been used, such as stones, beads, buttons or embroidery.

In England, the earliest glass eyes known were set into the wooden dolls of the late 17th century and they were dark brown and without pupils. Later ones are found with painted enamel eyes.

The first sleeping dolls were English and seem to have appeared about 1825. The eyes are joined by a bridge of wax that has a short wire loop sticking out of it. This loop is attached to a long length of string or wire that goes down through the neck and torso to emerge about the waist. This can be worked by hand from under the skirts.

About 1870 a more elaborate sleeping doll was invented and the eyes were made to close by a counter-balance action with a lead weight so that, when the doll was laid down, the weight fell backwards and the eyeballs moved in a downward direction so that only the lids were visible. The eyeballs are round and made of blown glass and are attached by metal wires to the lead weight. They are joined together behind with a bridge of putty covered in wax and the front of the eyeball is half dipped into wax to form the eyelid, lashes being put into place before the final dip.

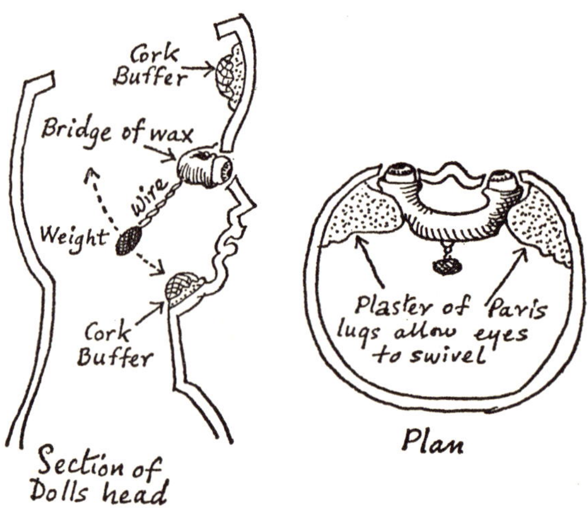

Fig. 9

This structure is placed into plaster of paris sockets on either side of the eyes and is thus loosely held into a position that only allows it to swivel through a narrow arc. To ensure the right amount of swing and therefore the amount of eye that should be seen, two cork buffers are glued into the inside of the head, one just above and between the eyes, the other lower down, in the throat, to stop the lead weight from hitting the delicate structure of the head, Occasionally a strip of wood glued across the top of the head serves a similar purpose.

Not surprisingly, many children have poked the eyes to see how they work, with the result that the lids are scratched and the lashes half missing. The simplest way to achieve a good repair is to take the whole eye system out of the head by chipping away the plaster of paris from one side to free the whole unit.

If the lashes and the lids are too far gone for patching, then it is as well to clear them away entirely and this you can do with a small sharp knife or lancet.

New lids are simple enough, but new lashes are something of a problem and will almost inevitably require several attempts —but, with experience, it can at last be done.

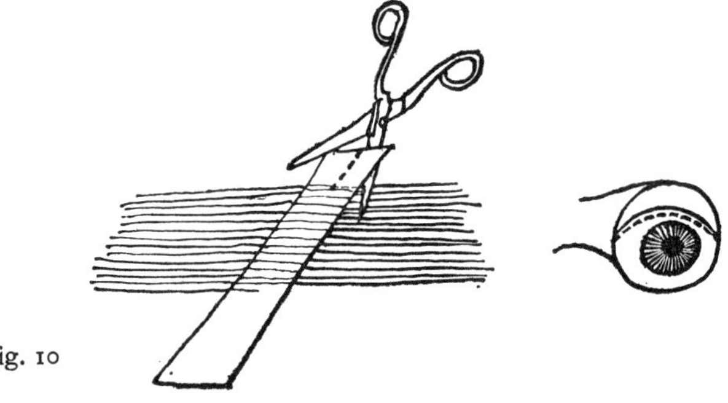

Fig. 10

I do it in the following manner: I cut a piece of my own hair, the straighter the hair the better, about one inch long and thick enough to make the lashes for one eye. This I lay flat on the table and across the centre of it I firmly press a strip of $\frac{1}{4}''$ wide Sellotape. I cut this strip of Sellotape along its centre and so make a pair of matching eyelashes.

I then squeeze a thread of glue in a curve above the iris of the eye and gradually lay on to it the strip of Sellotape and eyelash. When the glue hardens, the lashes can be trimmed with scissors. A much easier way to add eyelashes is to buy the ready-made false ones which are sold at the chain stores for 3*s.* 6*d.* and 5*s.* 9*d.* a pair. It is better to apply them after the eyes are in position, or the lashes may become caught and bent while the eyes are being eased into the sockets. They have their own tube of adhesive and when they are firmly glued they can be trimmed to the right shape.

To replace the eyelid, I give it a coat of tempera colour, using white, red and yellow and applying it rather thickly, and this too must be allowed to dry, which doesn't take very long. Now the eyelid has to be dipped into molten wax that is not *too* hot, and great care must be taken to allow the wax to reach only to the edges of the eyelashes.

A small doll has no need of eyelashes, so here you can paint the lid with tempera and then dip the whole into wax, removing the superfluous section afterwards with a knife. This, incidentally, is a most effective technique.

Old glass eyes are now hard to come by and if you cannot get them from the dolls' hospitals, friends, or dealers then you will unfortunately have to resort to modern plastic eyes. These can have their lids dipped in wax and their over-stiff and bushy eyelashes trimmed to match the older doll.

Painted eyes are more simply restored, assuming a steady hand and some skill with a fine sable brush. You will have to select the type of paint appropriate for the task; for shiny or metal eyes, an enamel paint or artists' oil paint that can be varnished; and for eyes that have a mat surface, tempera paint. The latter is far easier to handle and allows the finest lines to be drawn.

Eyes that are merely dull and dirty can be worked over with a bit of cotton wool on the end of a sharpened matchstick and the lids cleaned with a wax polish or face cream.

Metal eyes are improved by cleaning with the smallest possible drop of machine oil.

The Wig

The hair of most old dolls has enjoyed the most severe punishment, for it has been washed, curled, cut and then either pulled off or left to tangle. Since the beginning of the last century, wigs have been made from wool, silk, flax, thread, string, horsehair, cowhair, goathair, sheep's wool, yak, mohair, embroidery floss and nylon. All these materials have been in constant use, but the hair style and manner of construction have changed with the fashion of the day. It is therefore imperative to consult fashion magazines and reference books before repairing or replacing a wig.

Whenever possible, it is preferable to keep the old wig, and this can be washed after some experiment with a small section. It is as well to remember that the older glues are usually soluble in water so you will have to avoid an excess of wet at the roots.

Hair can be dry-cleaned with the shampoo sold for use on dogs, or with the powder sold at most chemists as light magnesium. This you should leave in the hair for some five minutes and then brush out.

Hot bran can also be used in just the same way.

Some hair can be curled as human hair is curled, with reasonably cool curling tongs, but not with 'permanent wave' materials, and it can be dampened with eau de Cologne or a little hair spray, and curled on small rollers.

Should only a portion of the original wig remain, then it may be arranged round the face and a hat or bonnet attached permanently to the crown of the head.

Fig. 11. Wigs

Fig. 12. Wigs

At first glance, I have often considered that nylon hair would do very well, but after it has been on the doll for some time, I invariably grow dissatisfied and get rid of it. Perhaps this is a similar problem to that of plastic flowers, which I find acceptable only when they set out to be something in their own right—such as unreal and imaginary growths that are decorative but do not attempt to deceive you into thinking them real.

I have found human hair superior to all the other materials for wig-making—and children's hair the best of all.

Straight hair is the easier to manage, but curly hair will look splendid if you can manage to make the wig with all the curls flowing in the right direction. I am grateful to get hair from any source but especially grateful if I am able, without offence, to ensure that it has been recently washed. It is almost impossible to wash it afterwards and, even if you do manage it, it never regains the natural gloss of living hair. I find that more and longer hair is needed to make wigs than might be imagined for a lot is cut to waste.

Wooden dolls, when they had hair at all, could boast only the simplest of wigs—a lump of hair glued directly on to the head or stitched on to a piece of cloth that was glued or nailed on to the head.

Wax dolls, particularly those of the early 19th century, would have their hair pushed into a slit in the top of the head and held in place with crescent-shaped pieces of stiff glued paper, a practice that often cracked the face below.

In the middle of the last century, the Pierotti and Montinari families were making some of the most beautiful and elaborate wax dolls imaginable and the care and skill lavished on the wigs was such as now to appear barely credible.

The Montinari dolls have each hair inserted singly into the wax. A hole was made with a hot needle and the hair placed into it so that it would 'grow' in the right direction. Further realism was achieved by spacing the hairs more widely apart as they got closer to the face and neck.

The Pierottis inserted small sections of hair into cuts in the wax and secured them by pressure from heated rollers. These groups of hairs would get closer together as they neared the crown.

I have tried both these techniques and found the first quite practicable but heartbreakingly tedious, whilst the second method worked very well. I used a small sharply pointed 'Balsa' knife and heated it on an electric ring. I held each group of hairs in my left hand, trimmed them with scissors into a straight line, made a small slit in the scalp with the heated knife, inserted the lock of hair, rewarmed the knife and with it pressed the flap of wax back into place.

The result would withstand hard pulling, but the most difficult part was to get the hair growing in the right direction and hanging naturally.

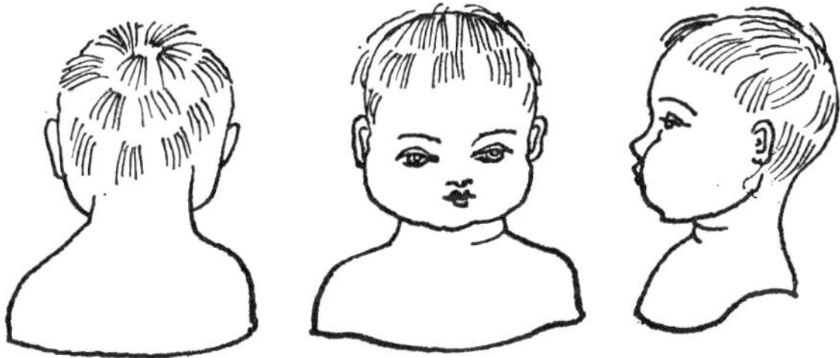

Fig. 13. Hair insertions for baby doll

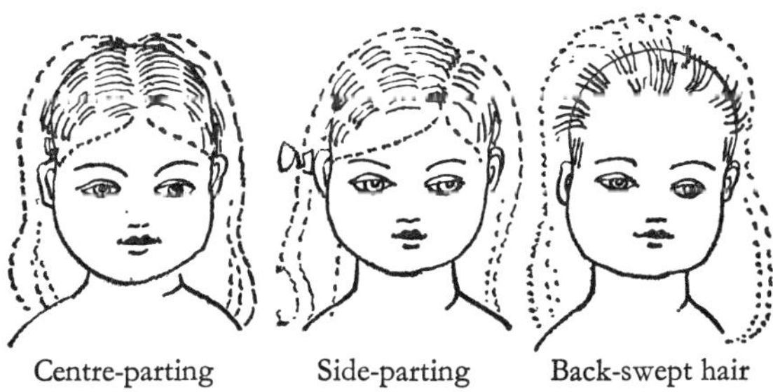

Centre-parting Side-parting Back-swept hair

I have drawn plans for such hair insertions: for a baby doll; for one with a fringe, a centre parting and a backward swept hair style.

Cheaper wax dolls had wigs similar to the bisque dolls, which were usually made up on a canvas foundation and glued to the top of the head, or inserted into a hole on the top of the head.

Bisque and Composition dolls are usually found to have wigs of human hair, Tibetan goat hair or mohair, made up in a variety of ways. The bisque heads have, more often than not, a large opening in the top of the head which serves to reduce the weight (they were taxed at one time by weight) and to make the insertion of eyes and teeth considerably easier. The holes are covered with a dome of strawboard or cork, to which the wig is glued, and as this part of the head is so often lost I have tried several ways of making new ones. Papier-mâché proved the most successful material and I have described its manufacture and use in the chapter dealing with bodies (see pages 49–51).

To find a suitable mould, I measure the opening and then search the house, armed with a ruler, until I find some cup or bowl of the right size.

If I use the laminated papier-mâché, I make it twice as thick as normal, about sixteen layers, and of newspaper rather than tissue, for the dome has to withstand harder treatment than any other part of the doll. A more professional result can be obtained with pulped papier-mâché, but the manner of construction is the same. If you grease the inside of the mould and press the papier-mâché into this to about $\frac{1}{4}''$ thick and leave it to dry, it will leave the mould quite readily and you will be able to trim the edges with scissors and make a small round hole in the top, if you need such a hole for the wig.

When cutting the lower edge of the dome, make it a little larger than necessary so that you can snip round and turn it

Fig. 14

inwards to make a flat surface that glues comfortably to the bisque.

You have to make a decision now about the style of wig and that will obviously depend upon the materials available and suitable and on the size of the doll. Human hair is rather coarse for a very small doll and I have often thought the styles chosen for new and restored dolls have been rather too adult and complicated for their subjects.

A traditional manner of construction is to twist strands of hair to two matching threads, rather as one would make a fringe.

A softer material than human hair is easier to manage, but if you do use human hair, then it will look particularly beautiful, and you will need a lot of it. I begin by cutting the hair into lengths a little more than twice as long as I want on the finished wig, remembering that the hair on the crown must be longer than that at the nape of the neck if it is all to finish up the same length.

Then I take a piece of stiff card about 12″ wide and round this I tie two pieces of thread to match the hair, about ½″ apart.

I cut lengths of hair into locks and, starting with the larger ones, I weave them through the threads.

Leaving half the lock hanging, I take the end under the bottom thread, over the top thread, then sloping to the right and down and over the bottom thread, up again over the top thread, down and under the bottom thread—and that is one lock completed.

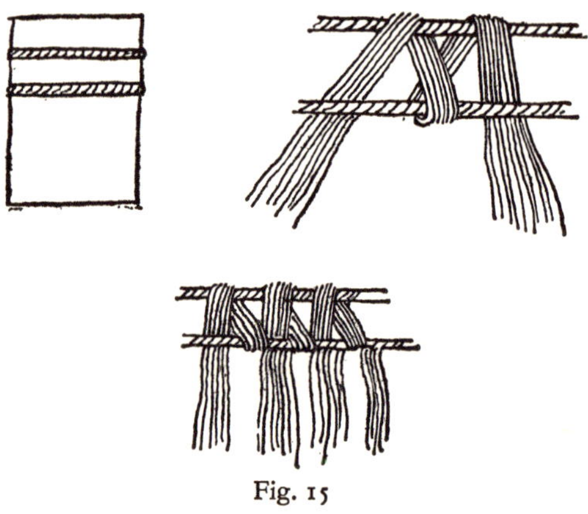

Fig. 15

This pattern I continue with more locks until I have a fringe big enough to form the complete wig.

Now I make a canvas skull-cap to fit the papier-mâché crown and on to it I sew the lengths of threaded hair in a spiral pattern that starts at the lower edge with the shorter locks and finishes at the top centre—with such variations as I see fit for different hair styles. In addition to this I sometimes fix an extra length of hair into the hole in the top to make the whole look thicker. To make this I take a bunch of hair, fold it in the middle and tie very tightly near to the fold. I then push it through the hole and glue it tightly into position so that I can spray out the hairs and smooth them over the rest of the wig. Many old dolls have inferior hair that is covered by such a topknot of good quality material.

Sometimes a very small doll may have a wig made only from a topknot of fine soft hair. To do this, dip the knot into the glue, hold the hairs firmly, put through the hole, and then glue the hairs lightly to the side of the head.

Fig. 16

With human hair I have had the best results from the following method. Take a very narrow strip of tape, dye it to match the hair, and cut it to reach from the forehead to the crown, plus 1″ or 2″, depending on the size of the doll; lay it on a flat surface and cover with glue (I find 'Evostick' very good); spread the hair across, with the tape in the centre (or at the side for a side parting) to cover the tape thinly and evenly.

When the glue is dry, stitch one or two rows along the tape, using matching cotton on the sewing machine, and with the hair uppermost. (See Fig. 17.)

Glue this to the crown and fold the extra 1″ or 2″ under at the back to make the hair fall evenly about the head.

Although I have tried many substitutes for human hair I have found none to match the reality, although some are more easily managed and have their special place in wig making.

Dolls' hair can be bought at Dryad Handicrafts, Northgates, Leicester, and 22, Bloomsbury St., London, W.C.1, quite reasonably priced, but in harsh and unnatural colours and far too wavy. The waves can be modified by wetting the

Fig. 17

strands of hair and tying a weight to one end whilst hanging up to dry. Although cold water dyes do not take well, a little dark brown is enough to modify the rather custard-yellow blonde. A similar hair called crêpe hair is sold in theatrical shops, and it is useful for stylised dolls—adults, Grannies and Pedlars. For such grey-haired dolls, I have used the bits of sheep's wool that I have picked up on the fells, particularly the long coarse strands from their tails. I have a French doll with a reddish-brown wig that I suspect to be cow hair, again from the tail, for it is very coarse, with a slight wave, and only suitable for such a large doll.

Embroidery floss serves very well for very small dolls and models, for it is easy to use and it is supplied in a good range of colours.

For middle-sized dolls, I have occasionally taken curls from sheepskin rugs. These are often long, hold together well and can be washed and brushed, preferably before they are cut from the skin. This wool I spread out as evenly as possible

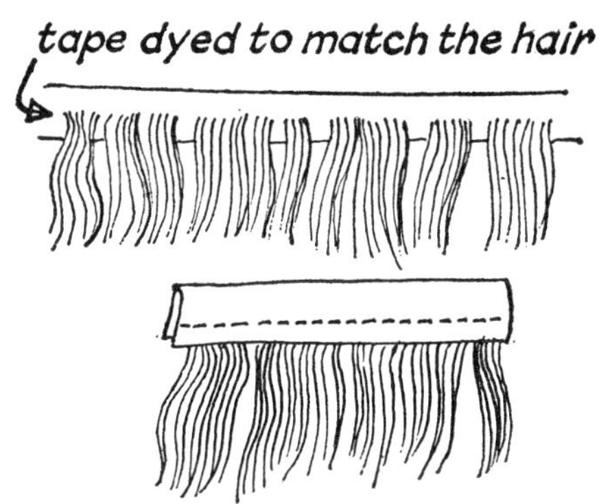

Fig. 18

along the lower half of a glued tape that matches the colour of the wool. I then fold the tape over and secure with two rows of stitching.

I have not found any fur suitable for a naturalistic wig. When the hairs have been long enough, the skin has been too thick to mould to the skull. Nevertheless, it is most useful for the un-naturalistic doll, such as the golliwog.

Recently in Croydon I saw a hairdresser's shop displaying doll-sized wigs made of real hair. These would be excellent for a very special doll, and I believe that in America it is possible to buy all kinds of wigs for dolls, and they may well soon be available in this country.

The Body

Although dolls have been made of clay, bone, stone and pottery, I do not consider their repair comes within the scope of this book, belonging as they do more to the world of archaeology than any other. I shall therefore confine myself to those dolls' bodies made of wood, leather, wax, china, cloth and composition.

Wooden Dolls

The better quality wood dolls are made of willow, which is reasonably easy to carve, does not splinter and sandpapers well, whilst the cheaper 'Dutch Dolls' were usually made from fir, and quite roughly finished. The common damage is broken joints and lost limbs, though woodworm must be checked, as described in the first chapter. When a variety of timber is not available to you, it is a good plan to take the doll to a shop that sells wooden dowelling, or to a timber yard, and

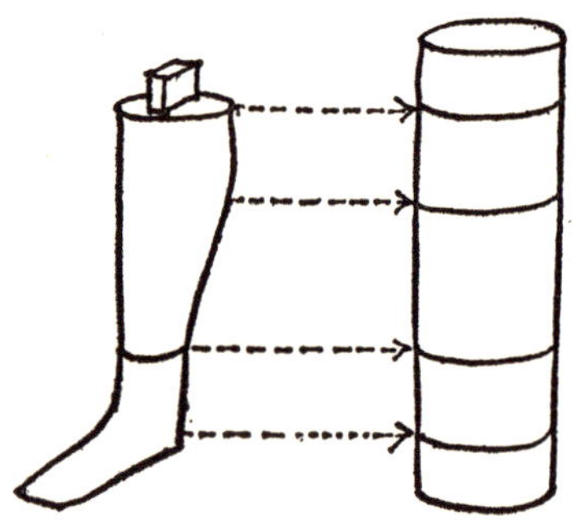

Fig. 19

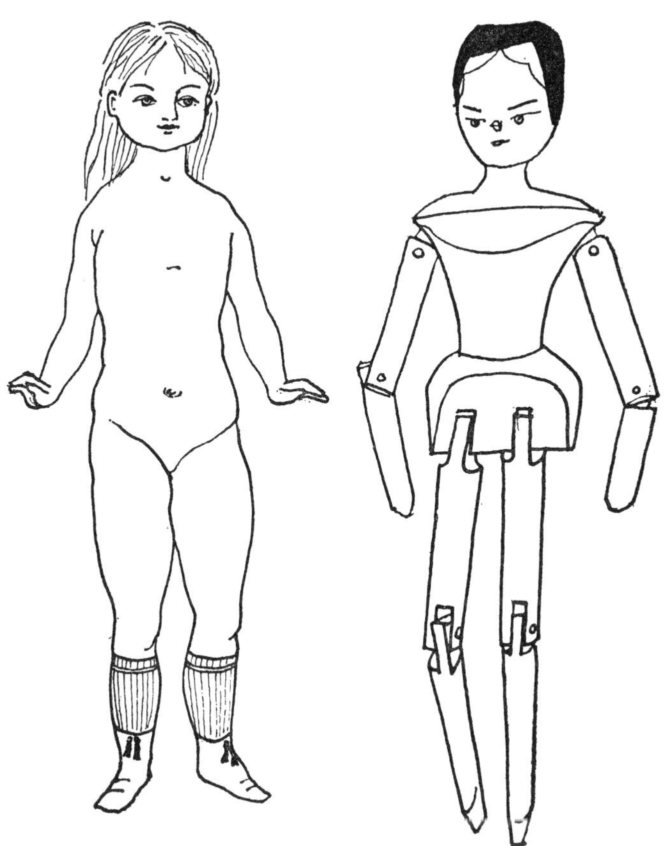

Frozen Charlotte
China doll made in one piece
without movable joints

'Dutch Doll'
Carved wooden doll
with wooden joints

Fig. 20

look amongst their stock for the timber that will match your doll, choosing dowelling of a diameter equal to the thickest part of the limb you need, or the length of the foot, whichever is the greater. You will need a good sharp knife and a variety of grades of sandpaper.

To match up a leg where one is missing you can put your dowelling alongside the original and mark off features, such as the widest point, ankle, top of the foot and so on. (Fig. 19).

As you carve, these marks will be lost and so you must keep comparing and re-marking as you go along; and don't forget that you are making a pair, not a replica, so that the feet and hands will have to be left and right. Once the limb has been carved, it is easier to paint it before attaching it to the body.

Hip joints usually consist of flat flanges of wood on the top of the thighs that fit into slots in the lower half of the torso. These are held into place, and allowed to swivel, by a wooden pin.

A similar wooden shaft goes through the chest and shoulders and the arms are pinned to that in such a way that they can swivel one way.

Stuffed Bodies

A great many of the dolls surviving from the last century have stuffed bodies. Their covering is of leather, cotton or American cloth and they are filled with such materials as sawdust, rag, wood-wool, hay, cork, bran and hair. I opened one recently to find it inexplicably full of lentils!

The modern rag dolls are filled with such washable materials as kapok and Terylene.

Some of the older dolls will have only the torso stuffed, whilst the lower limbs are made of wood, composition or china. Some will have no movement at the joints, and others will be sufficiently elaborately equipped to enjoy a freedom of

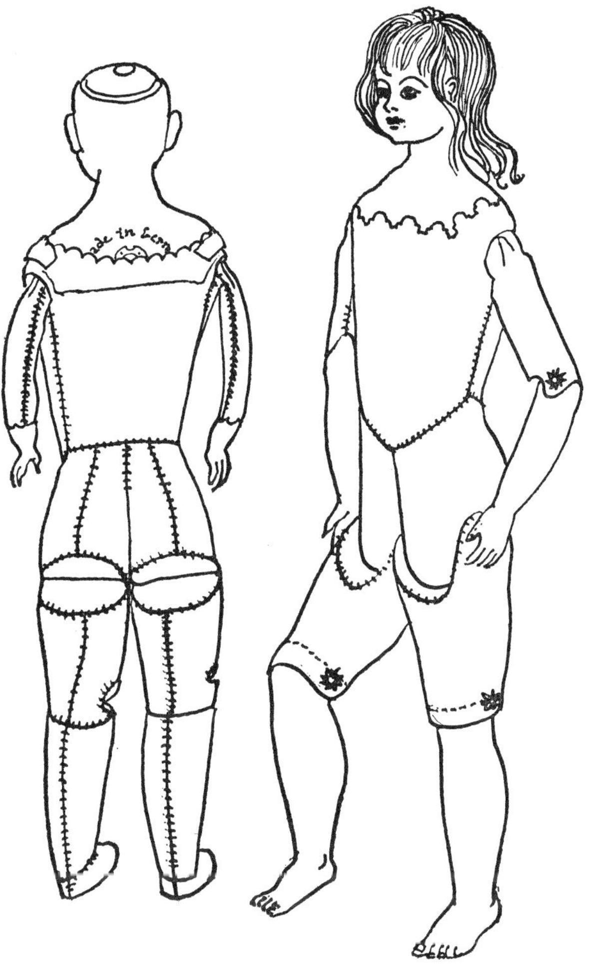

Bisque Doll
Leather body with gussets

Bisque Doll
Leather body with hinged joints

Fig. 21

Bisque Doll
Composition body with
ball and socket joints

Wax Doll
Cloth body with
stitched joints

Fig. 22

movement only surpassed by those made of wood and jointed in the manner of an artist's lay figure.

Occasionally one may acquire a head and shoulders that have lost their body and, as I consider it worth while to make a whole new body, I will go on to describe the construction, with patterns, of a simple stuffed body.

The size must first be determined by comparison with others of the era. The later the doll, the larger the head in proportion to the body, except in the case of those grown-up 'Fashion dolls', where the fashionable ideals of the time were followed, the aim being primarily to sell clothes. The limbs of Victorian dolls were usually small, and the hands and feet quite comically tiny, presumably because of the widely held ideal of the delicate lady, whose small hands and feet were so much admired.

Presumably those of our own era will eventually be described as having very long legs, or in some cases quite remarkable bosoms.

This general purpose pattern (Fig. 23) is intended to be adaptable for a wide variety of dolls, from a very young child to an adult.

The bodies are usually made of a strong, closely woven cotton that will last well, hold its shape and contain fine particles of stuffing, but should you wish to make one of leather, then you will require the very soft kid known as skiver. Such fine kid will have thinner areas that are too delicate to use, and these you must identify and avoid when cutting out the pattern. It may also repay you to take the paper patterns with you when buying the leather so that you can lay them out and choose the most economical piece. It may be sewn by machine, using a medium-to-large stitch. The small stitch would allow it to tear away.

First stitch the long seams, but leave an opening free to allow access for the stuffing.

To prevent a long body bending in the middle, a piece of wooden dowelling may be introduced.

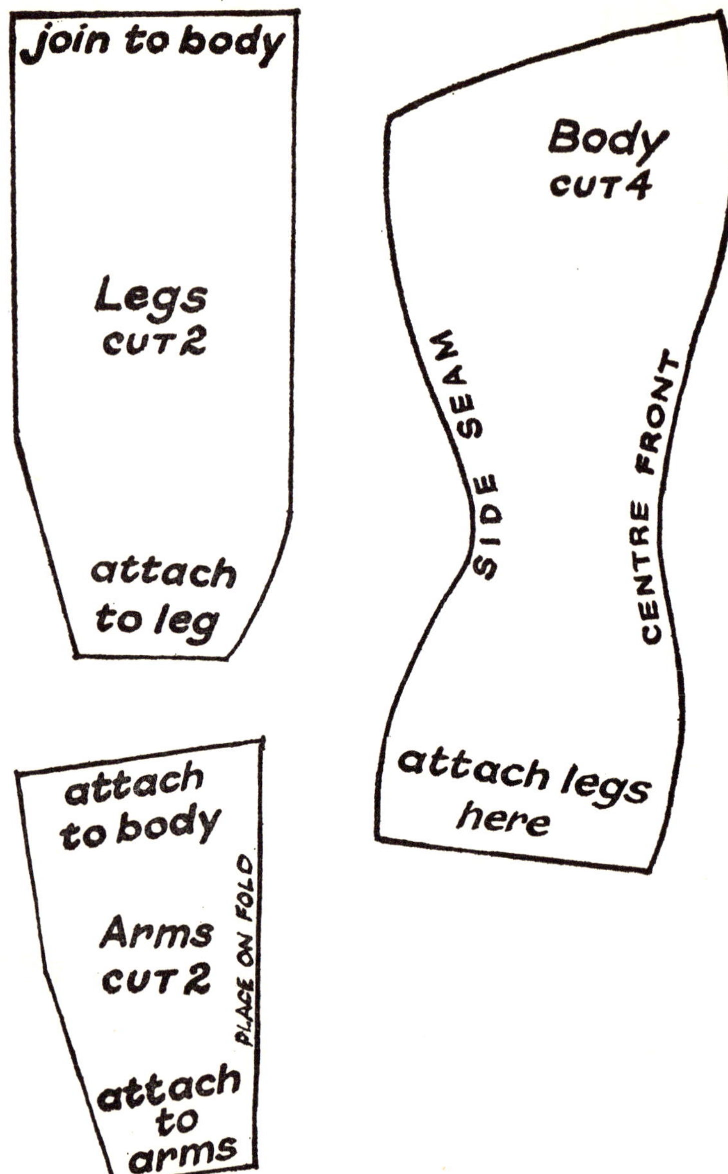

Fig. 23. Pattern for stuffed body for 20″ doll. Drawn to scale ½″ to 1″

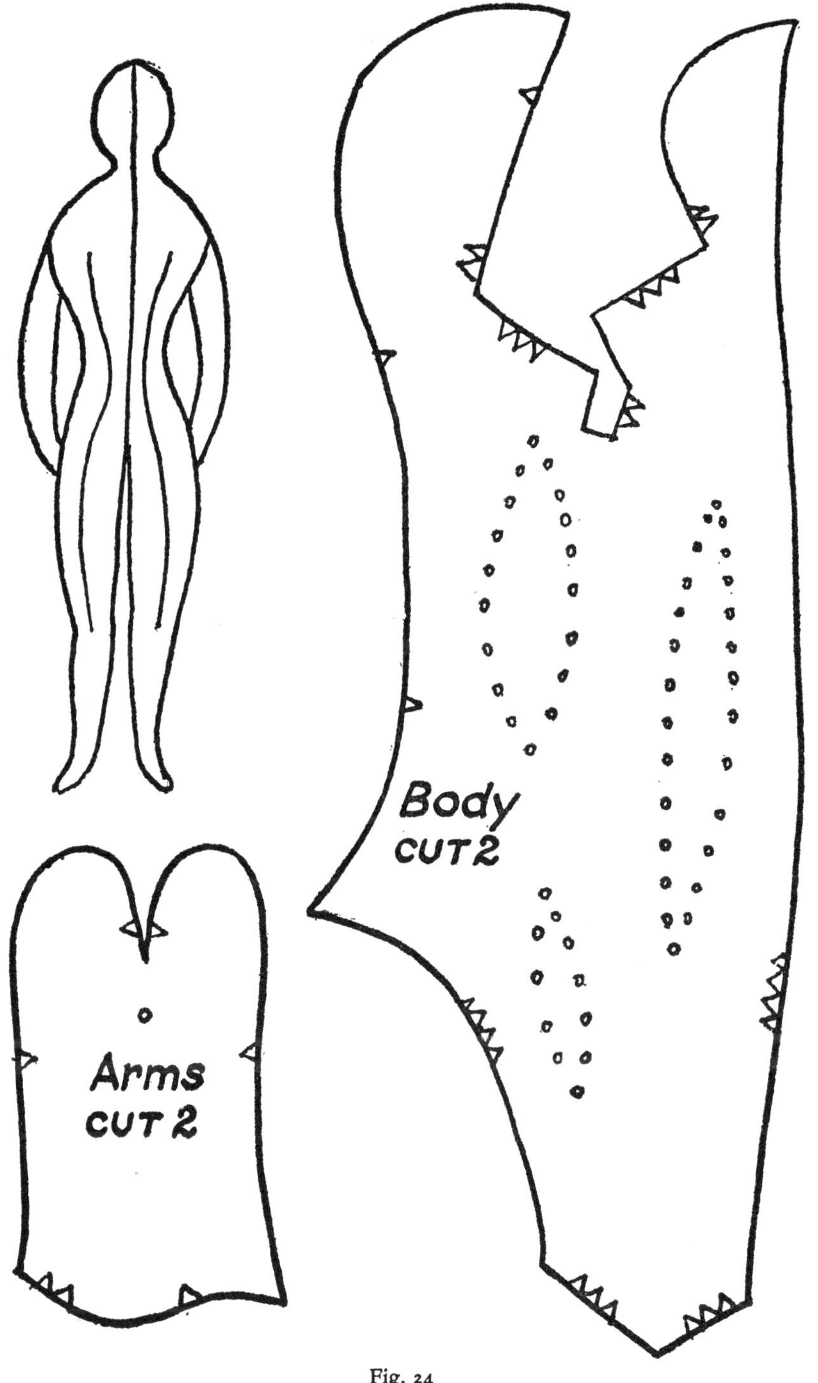

Fig. 24

The stuffing can be of any of the materials I have already mentioned and should be rammed firmly into place with a rod.

The second pattern (Fig. 24) is drawn from an old Victorian pattern for a rag doll. Like so many Victorian things it is a little over-complicated, but it makes an interestingly shaped doll that could only be from that era, and I included it for no other reason. I own a very worn kid body with a broken Meissen head, which is a very similar shape. The pattern I have drawn makes a doll about 6½″ high and is very fiddling to make so small as this.

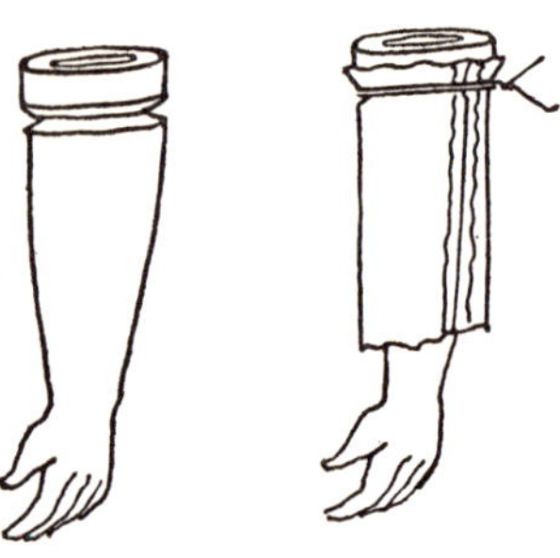

Fig. 25

In the case of limbs, the top seams are left open for stuffing and if part of these limbs (such as the forearms) are of solid material, there is usually a ridge that allows the cloth or leather to be tied with strong linen thread, turned inside out and stuffed from the top.

These extremities may be carved from wood, as already described in the earlier section on wooden dolls, or modelled, as described in the next chapter.

Should you find such carving beyond your skill, then I would advise you to make them in cloth or leather and dress the doll in long clothes.

The forearms and hands of old dolls are very often made of leather, usually white, but occasionally red or yellow, to look like gloves. Having just repaired such hands, I found that the best thing to do was to unstitch the forearm from the arm, empty out the stuffing and repair the breaks from behind with adhesive plaster (sold by that name in chemists' shops).

In America, there are several dolls' hospitals that sell china limbs of many kinds and sizes, beautifully made and most decorative, but I know of no such manufacture in England as yet.

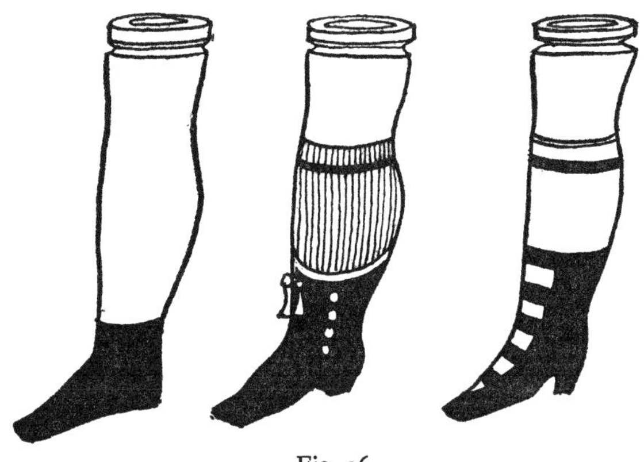

Fig. 26

Restringing and Restoring Dolls with Composition Bodies

The ball-and-socket jointed dolls are usually made of composition, or wood and composition, and may be composed of as many as seventeen pieces. The body, arms and legs are hollow to take the strands of elastic, whilst the hands and feet are solid.

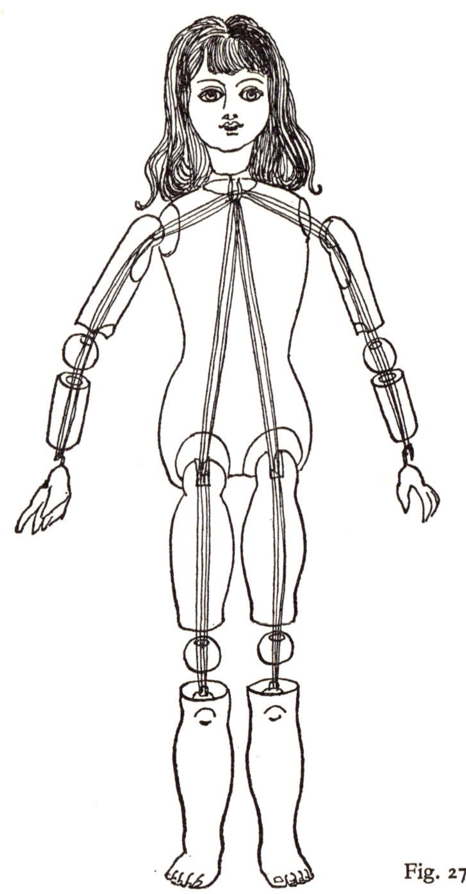

Fig. 27

Figure 27 shows the stringing of a 10″ Simon Halbig doll made in 1915. It took $1\frac{1}{2}$ yards of round elastic to re-string. (Three different thicknesses of round elastic can be bought at the Altrincham Rubber Co., The Downs, Altrincham, Cheshire: 1*s*., 6*d*. and 3*d*. per yard, plus postage.)

First, measure from the hook on the lower leg joint to the neck of the doll and cut a piece of elastic twice this length for each leg. Then measure the length of both arms, plus the width of the body, and cut a piece twice this length, but in both cases add a few inches to make it possible to tie a knot. It is a help to have a length of wire longer than the doll's body, and with a hook at one end, to lead the elastic through the body.

Start restringing by passing the elastic through the wire hook on one of the knee joints and bringing both ends through the hollow thighs and body to knot and hook on to the neck hook. Both arms are on the one piece of elastic that runs through the shoulders and chest. The major problem is one of tension, for the limbs must move freely without being loose and gangling.

Simple cracks and dents in composition dolls can be filled with Polyfilla, sanded smooth and painted, but when a part is lost you can carve or model a replacement out of that particularly useful material 'Plastone'.

Hands can be modelled in solid Plastone round a metal hook, and odd fingers made to glue to the old hand. A leg can be modelled around a cardboard roll and of course all these can be sanded when dry and painted to match the original.

Alternatively such replacements can be of papier-mâché so I will, at this point, describe two ways of making it.

Laminated Papier-mâché

For this you will need tissue paper in two colours and flour-paste of a fairly thick consistency. It should be home-made flour-paste, rather than the various pastes sold for decorators, to avoid unwelcome additives.

Grease the object you wish to copy with Vaseline or face cream. Cut the tissue into small 1″ squares, or triangles for rounded shapes. Dip these into the paste and apply to the model, overlapping somewhat until it is all covered. Repeat with another coat in a different colour of tissue (the colour change is to ensure a full coverage), until about eight layers have been achieved. Stroke each layer with your fingers as you go, to render the joins invisible.

Dry, over a stove or in the airing-cupboard, and then rub smooth with very fine sandpaper, for, with drying, it will have developed fine wrinkles. To get a finer finish, a few thin coats of gesso may be applied.

The grease will allow the removal of the papier-mâché from its mould, but, if it is in the round, it may have to be cut free and rejoined by a further application of pasted tissue.

Papier-mâché made with Pulped Paper

This is made of paper, whiting and glue and is used in the same way as modelling clay.

The paper must be very absorbent, so that pastel paper is ideal, although newspaper is quite good, easy to manage and, of course, easy to come by.

Tear into the smallest possible shreds (no larger than 1″), and soak overnight in water, taking care that all get saturated. The following day the water is poured away and the paper broken down to a pulp, by rubbing and beating until it is fine enough to be quite free from lumps. I found the liquidiser on my electric food mixer pulped it beautifully and effortlessly, a breakfastcupful at a time, plus rather a lot of water to save jamming. Now all the water must be removed by putting the pulp into a cloth and wringing it hard. I found that two sheets of newspaper made a ball of pulp almost as big as a tennis ball, and when making this amount I added about two dessertspoons full of whiting and enough flour-paste to make it the right consistency for modelling—that is, free of lumps and readily malleable.

Using this like modelling clay, you can make limbs which

you can harden by leaving to dry out in a very slow oven, before sanding and painting.

This pulp can be cast in a mould instead of modelled, to make a hollow limb. A simple little mould can be made of plaster, laminated papier-mâché, or even modelling clay (e.g. pressed on to a doll's body and cut into two halves and then allowed to dry).

The pulp is pressed into this mould until it is a reasonable thickness and dried in a slow oven before the mould is cut away.

This method gives a better surface than modelled papier-mâché and an even finer surface may be achieved by the three coats of gesso and a final painting with egg tempera or Cryla colours such as I have described in an earlier section (page 17).

Flexible Moulds

Various compounds are now sold made from vinyl resins that can be used to make flexible moulds time and time again, for after use they can be melted down. Because of the heating they are unsuitable for making moulds of composition or wax dolls, but are excellent for clay, plasticine, china, wood, metal, etc. The one I have used is called Vinatex (made by Vinatex Ltd., Devonshire Road, Carshalton, Surrey). It is made in three grades, with different melting ranges and flexibilities, from soft to very hard. I have used the standard range red compound to cast limbs for some of my dolls. Plasticine, clay or china can be used without treatment, but porous materials, such as plaster and wood, require a coat of shellac (20–30 parts of T.N. shellac to 100 parts of methylated spirit), to save them from absorbing the compound. The simplest method of casting is to put the object (in this case a leg) on a horizontal surface such as a tin lid and surround it with a retaining wall of oiled paper high enough to hide the leg. The oiled paper can be held in place with clay or Plasticine.

The Vinatex has to be heated very slowly in a vessel of aluminium, stainless steel or tin (not zinc or copper) and it is necessary to heat it *so* slowly that you may need an asbestos mat on top of the hotplate. Alternatively, you can heat it by hot air, standing one vessel inside another. At 200° C. it will be of a consistency to pour smoothly. It should be melted little by little and stirred continuously. Smoke or excessive smell shows that you are overheating it.

Pour the melted compound quickly and in a steady stream until the mould is filled, but do not pour it directly on to the model, but allow it to rise up round it, and in this way it will drive out the air bubbles. Allow the mould to cool slowly for several hours and the model can then be eased out by hand.

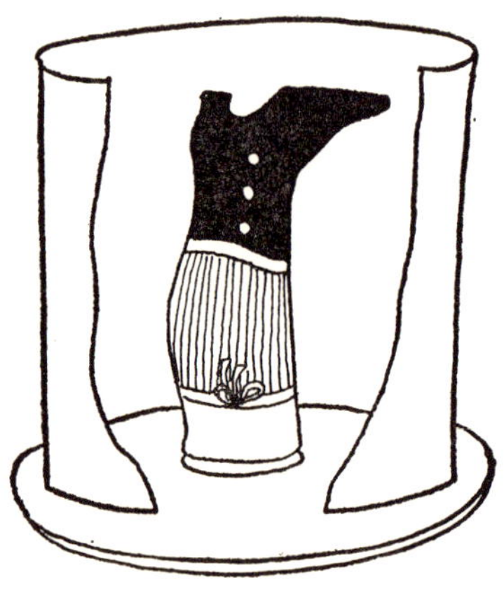

Fig. 27a

SECTION 2

Dressing the Doll

FEW DOLLS THAT survive from the last century have their original clothing in good condition, but fortunately even badly damaged clothes can be repaired—and the worst can at least be camouflaged.

When there are no clothes at all, then the problems are far greater, for there will have to be a choice of style and material before the actual fabrication of clothing.

It goes without saying that when the clothes are contemporary with the doll and attractive then they must at all costs be retained and refurbished; and, if some are missing, as they so often are, then these can often be supplied from chance sources or by their manufacture from old materials. The underclothes are often in better condition than the frocks, which can be very dirty, and all will look wonderfully better for careful cleaning and washing.

RESTORING THE ORIGINAL CLOTHES

CLEANING

Stains should be removed before washing and I list now such problems and solutions as I have encountered.

'Ironmould' can be removed from cotton and linen materials with salts of lemon or oxalic acid, sprinkled on to the stain and boiling water poured over it.

For woollens and silks, use hyposulphite bleach.

Scorch-marks, if not too bad, may be taken from linen and cotton with hypochlorite bleach, and from wool and silk with diluted hydrogen peroxide.

Rust can be treated with salts of sorrel.

Mildew is very difficult to get rid of, but for cotton and linen you can try hydrogen peroxide or salts of sorrel, whilst for wool and silk you will have to use permanganate of potash, which will stain it brown and oblige you to bleach it with hydrogen peroxide.

Ink stains can sometimes be removed with milk, but should that fail, cotton and linen clothes can be treated with lemon juice and salt, on to which boiling water is poured; and for silk you will again have to use potassium permanganate followed by hydrogen peroxide (1 part hydrogen peroxide, 1 part vinegar, 4 parts water).

Grease can be attacked with carbon tetrachloride, rubbing from the outer edges in to the centre, or by putting a pad of blotting-paper under the stain and then pressing with a warm iron to drive the grease through and out of the cloth.

Washing

Before you start, coloured clothes will have to be tested to see if the dye will run, and this can be done on some unimportant hidden patch by wetting and pressing on to a white cloth. Should the colour come off on to the white cloth, washing is inadvisable and the garment will have to be dry-cleaned professionally. (Very delicate old clothes are better left as they are.)

Linen and cotton, being strong and durable, can usually be washed in warm, soapy water, or with a detergent if the water is hard. If white garments still look grey they will stand a mild bleach and the finer cottons will be improved by being lightly starched. They may be pressed with a moderately hot iron.

Faded colours in cottons may be revived somewhat by adding salt to the final rinse.

Velveteen and corduroy, being both of cotton, may be

washed in warm, soapy water, but they should not be rubbed or wrung out—just left hanging to drip. Corduroy may be ironed from the back, but velveteen will have to be steamed.

Silk should be washed gently in lukewarm water and detergent, then rinsed in warm water, then in cold and finally, to bring back some natural spring to the fibres, rinsed in cold water to which has been added vinegar (1 teaspoonful to 2 pints). The silk should be dried on a towel and ironed from the back with a warm iron.

Long soaking, too hot water and soap can all cause the silk to yellow and, if this should happen, then it may be bleached with hydrogen peroxide (but not with chlorine.) Some lightweight silks are improved by a little stiffening with stationer's gum (1 to 4 teaspoons to each pint of water, depending on how stiff it needs to be).

Watered silk will lose its pattern if it is washed.

Wools do not always wash well, if at all, and some will need to be dry-cleaned; and even those that do wash, such as serge, flannel and nun's veiling, require careful handling if they are not to shrink. They should not be allowed to soak, and should be washed in lukewarm water and detergent. Squeeze out the water without wringing and shake from time to time, whilst drying, to fluff out the hairs. Do not dry with direct heat and, if you have to bleach, use hydrogen peroxide, for chlorine would only make it even yellower.

Lace should be treated as you would the material from which it is made.

All other materials will be better dry-cleaned, especially silk velvets, brocades, watered silks, materials with colouring that will run, and very fragile materials.

Small repairs may be effected in the customary way and when ribbons and buttons are added they should be of old material, silk or cotton, but never of nylon. New ribbon can be rapidly aged by washing it several times.

MAKING NEW CLOTHES FOR THE DOLL

The first essential for those who plan to dress dolls is a chest of drawers, or a set of cardboard boxes, to house every scrap of old cloth, fine material and miniature oddment that might one day prove useful. Friends may part with materials they have stored for years and never found as useful as they had once hoped. Old materials may be bought from market stalls and jumble sales and at auction sales (usually at the very end, with the other sad broken bits from the attic).

Old sheets and pillowcases will cut up into a great many underclothes. In addition to pieces of cloth, you will need to acquire ribbons, lace, very small buttons, tiny hooks and eyes, very narrow elastic, small beads, lengths of fine wire, feathers, the smallest artificial flowers, thin leather (such as an old glove), old straw and felt hats, old cotton and woollen vests, pieces of fur and any narrow tape; and any time you use a powdered dye, you can put a little aside to build up a selection to use later for dolls' clothes.

To know how to identify and how to choose the correct style of dress, you will need the help of fashion plates and illustrated history books and you cannot ever know enough of the visual detail of the era concerned. Such research has its pitfalls though, for the Godey fashion drawings are always so attractive that it is a great temptation to swallow them whole and so overdress a modest plaything. But such fashion plates do give you the fashionable silhouette of the time, perhaps the surest guide of any.

It is important to decide just how old your doll was supposed to be—a baby, a child or an adult—and this is best decided from the proportions rather than the features, which are so often misleading.

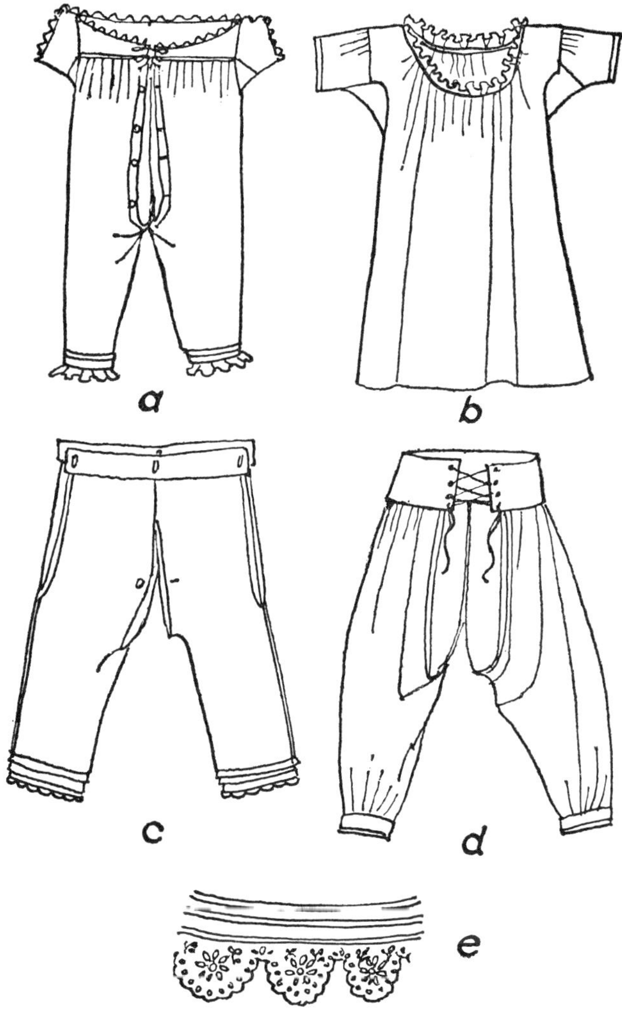

Fig. 28. Underclothes, 1800–1840

a. Cotton drawers about 1820. *b*. Cotton chemise about 1825. *c*. Cotton drawers about 1830. *d*. Cotton drawers about 1830. *e*. Detail of embroidery about 1830.

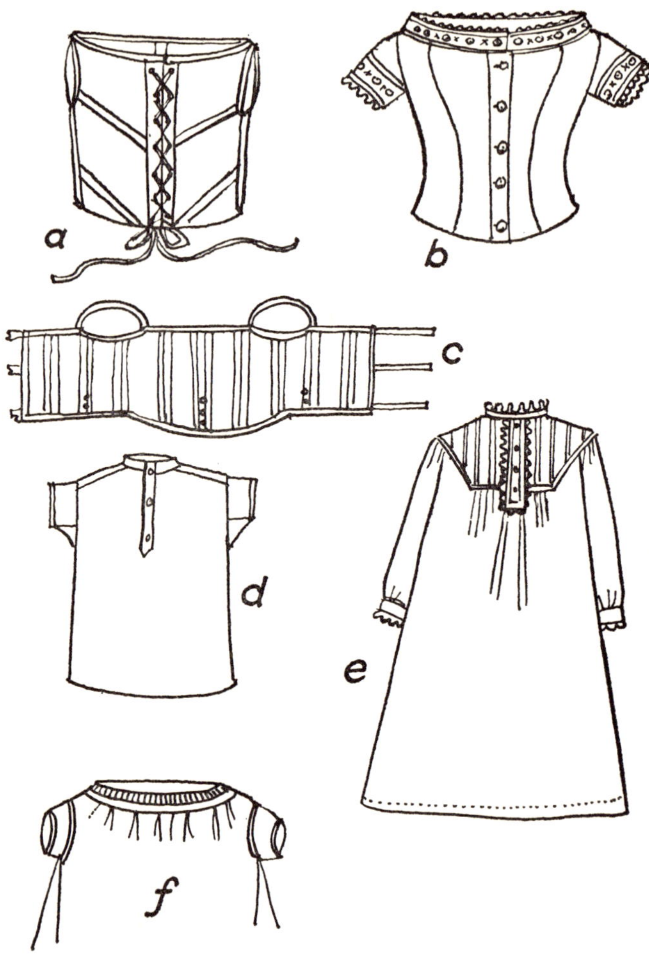

Fig. 29. Underclothes, 1850–1870

a. Child's stays about 1850. *b.* Child's bodice about 1860. *c.* Child's stays about 1870. *d.* Boy's flannel vest about 1870. *e.* Nightdress about 1870. *f.* Chemise about 1870.

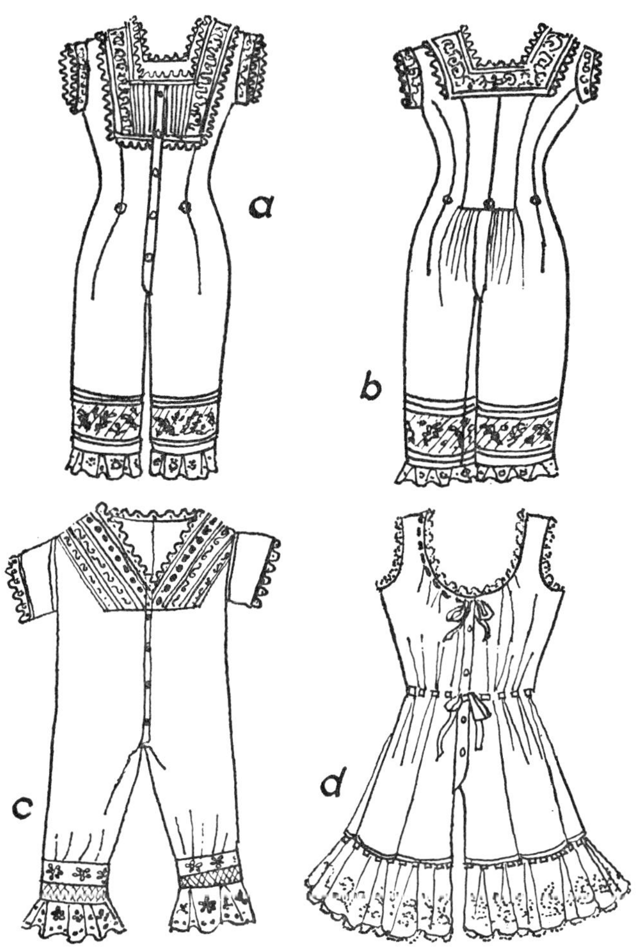

Fig. 30. Underclothes, 1880–1910

a. Chemise drawers, 1880. *b*. Chemise drawers, 1890. *c*. Cotton combinations, 1890. *d*. Cotton combinations, 1910.

Fig. 31. Underclothes, 1920–1960
a. Petticoat, 1920–1930. *b*. Vest, 1930–1950. *c*. Vest, 1930–1960. *d*. Petticoat, 1950. *e*. Vest, 1940–1960. *f*. Knickers, 1950–1960. *g*. Underpants, 1930–1960. *h*. Y-front underpants, 1940–1960.

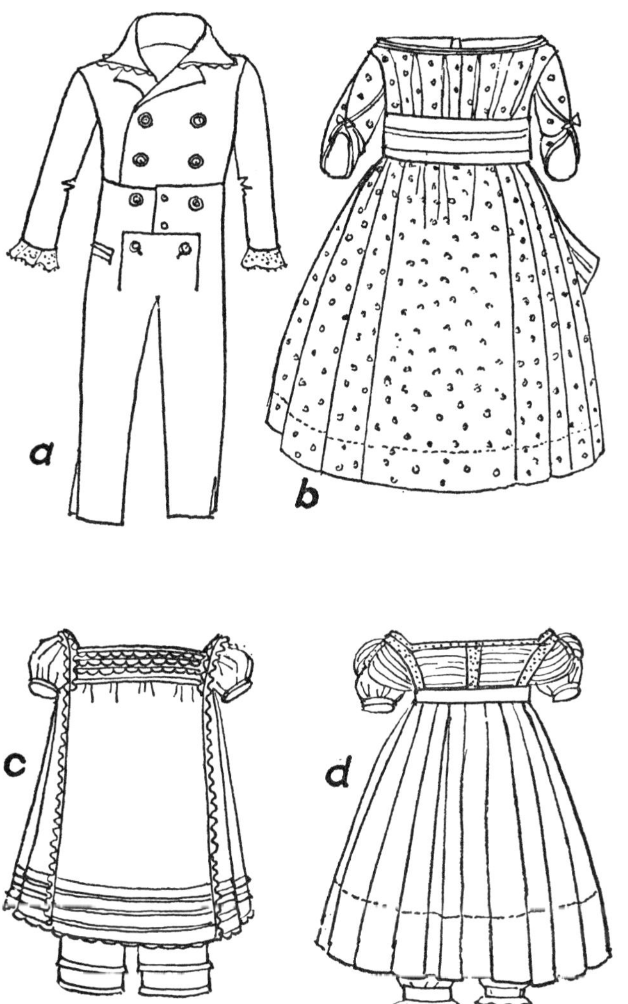

Fig. 32. Children's Clothes, 1800–1830
a.Boy's suit, 1810. *b*. Girl's dress, 1810. *c*. Boy's dress, 1820. *d*. Girl's dress, 1830.

Fig. 33. Children's Clothes, 1840–1870
a. Girl's dress, 1840. *b.* Boy's tunic dress, 1850. *c.* Girl's party dress, 1860. *d.* Boy's suit, 1870.

Fig. 34. Children's Clothes, 1880–1900
a. Girl's dress, 1880. *b*. Boy's suit, 1890. *c*. Boy's suit, 1900. *d*. Girl's dress, 1900

Fig. 35. Children's clothes, 1910–1940
a. Sailor suit, 1910. *b*. Boy's or girl's tunic dress, 1920. *c*. Kilt and jersey, 1930. *d*. Pinafore dress, 1940.

Fig. 36. Children's Clothes, 1950–1960
a. Girl's suit, 1950. *b.* Boy's suit, 1950. *c.* Boy's casual clothes, 1960. *d.* Girl's clothes, 1960.

Fig. 37. Children's Coats and Jackets, 1810–1843
a. Boy's jacket, 1810. *b*. Tippet, 1820. *c*. Boy's tunic (front), 1843. *d*. Boy's tunic (back), 1843. *e*. Boy's hat, 1843.

Fig. 38. Children's Coats and Jackets, 1860–1897
a. Girl's coat, 1860s. *b*. Girl's coat, 1880s. *c*. Girl's suit, 1896. *d*. Boy's middy jacket, 1897.

Fig. 39. Children's Coats and Jackets, 1920–1960
a. Baby's coat, 1920. *b.* Coat and leggings, 1924. *c.* Girl's coat, 1950. *d.* Duffle coat; boy or girl, 1950–1960. *e.* Anarak; boy or girl, 1950–1960.

I have occasionally seen a baby doll dressed up in clothes that only a rich, middle-aged matron would have chosen. The large head and tubby body of a child are quite unsuited to adult clothing and can give an unpleasantly stunted appearance.

As almost all the trimmings that have to be applied, such as laces, ribbons and buttons, are too large for the correct proportions of real life, any doll is in constant danger of being overdressed.

Once these knotty problems of period style and fashion have been decided, there will have to be a selection of materials, a choice that is dominated by the size of the doll and the difficulties of getting a fabric light enough to hang well, one that will not give the impression of a dress 2 inches thick! On the whole, cotton, silk, light-weight wool and fine lawn will lend themselves more readily to the solution of this problem than brocade, velvet and the heavy woven cloths. The modern man-made fabrics are to be avoided, for their valuable crease-resisting qualities are here a positive disadvantage. They will not hang well on a small figure and, when gathered, give a balloon effect.

The choice of colours will also have to relate to the complexion and hair of the doll itself and this problem I have always found best solved by trial and error, rather than by going firmly ahead with some rationalised or preconceived notion of what it ought to wear or what I would like for myself. The unlikely bit of cloth so often turns out to be the one that looks right when held against the doll.

An old doll should be dressed from the underclothes outwards and any garment that is intended to be a fitted garment should be tight. A doll wearing a lot of underclothes, and they wore a surprising amount in the 19th century, will look and feel much better than a thinly clad doll, which has a peculiarly hard and rigid feeling.

Fortunately it is a great deal easier to make clothes for a doll than it is for a child, for the former can be laid on the table and have its patterns made directly on to its surface, nor is there any need to allow the same fullness for movement.

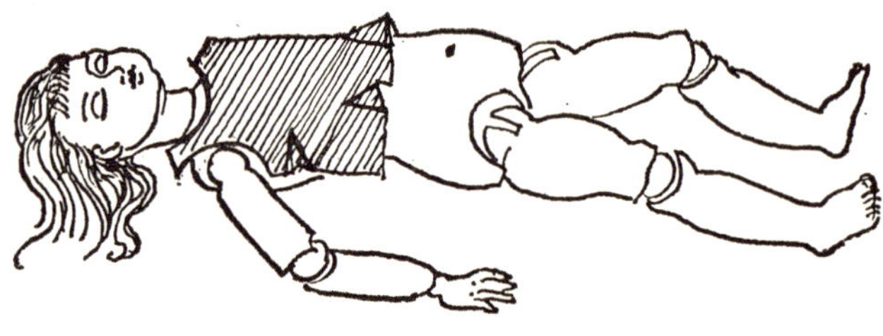

Fig. 40

I use newspapers to make my patterns, creasing, cutting and darting until it really fits the doll. The armholes and neck-holes can be cut as you press the paper on to the doll. The basic bodice patterns will usually look similar to the accompanying sketches. (Figs. 41 and 42.)

Such basic patterns are readily adapted to more complicated needs, as in the case of a pointed waistline on a bodice with tucking or pleats.

I use a softer paper for the sections of pattern that have to be gathered, such as the sleeves and skirt, and paper handkerchiefs are excellent, for they will gather and hang in much the same way as the actual cloth. They will even split in two layers if you need to simulate very fine gauze. Patterns made in this way will make no allowances for turnings and you must remember to allow for this when cutting out the clothes.

The dress will, in almost all cases, look the better for being lined, and it is helpful to pin the material to the lining before cutting out, and to make up the two materials together. Even a very small dress will look better for lining, but you must use a very fine lawn to do it.

FRONT
BODICE
BACK
BODICE
PLAIN
SLEEVE
PUFF
SLEEVE
BELL
SLEEVE
LEG OF
MUTTON
SLEEVE
TAILORED
SLEEVE
UPPER
PIECE
TAILORED
SLEEVE
UNDER
PIECE

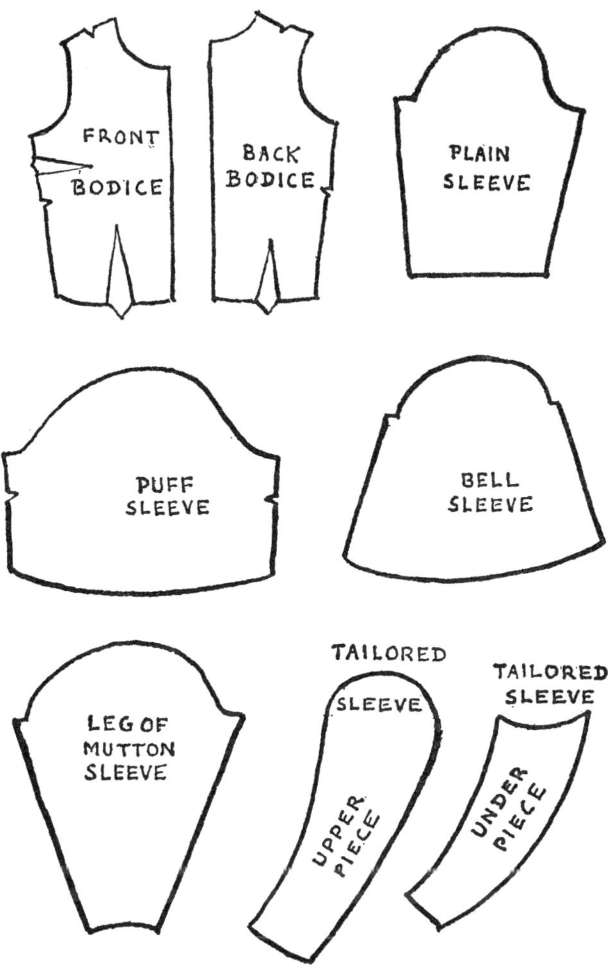

Fig. 41

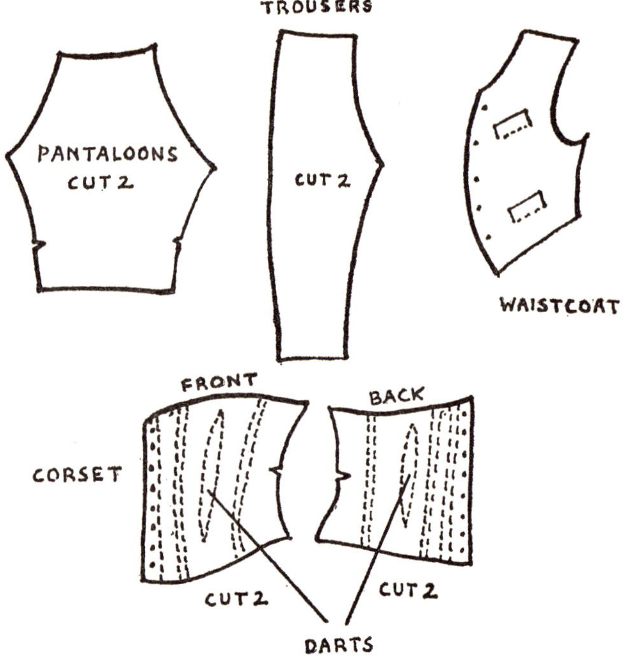

Fig. 42

All such dressmaking is in miniature and it is obvious that you should use only the smallest needles, the finest cotton or pure silk thread, and the smallest stitches.

STOCKINGS (Fig. 43)

Stockinette material will serve this purpose very well, such as old vests, or stockings of cotton, silk or wool, but not nylon for an old doll. Sometimes coarse lace can be used effectively.

To measure, wrap the material round the leg and tack together, stretching tightly as you go. Slip it off the leg and stitch along the line of tacking stitches with the sewing

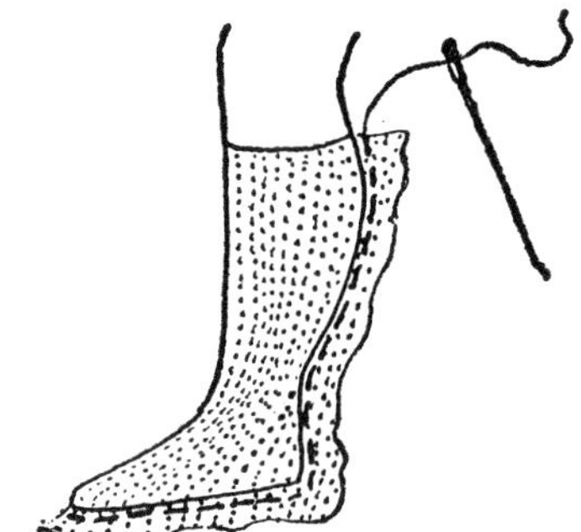

Fig. 43

machine. Cut away the surplus as close as possible, turn inside out and under at the top.

Boots and Shoes (Figs. 44 and 45)

Boots and shoes may be of leather, satin, silk, velvet or felt, although I have rarely considered the last to be very suitable for an old doll. I have an old French doll that retains its original felt shoes and, although I would not wish to replace them, I cannot but regard their material as an inappropriate choice.

When leather is used, it should be of the thinnest and, if possible, it should be old and worn. For this purpose, I have always found well-used kid gloves most suitable and fairly easy to obtain. Should you have to use new leather, then some semblance of age may be achieved by pulling, straining, stretching, rubbing on the floor, even staining and using every possible effort to make it look worn.

To make patterns for boots or shoes, draw round the doll's feet and then enlarge the shapes until they look like the characteristic shape of the footwear you have in mind, square-toed, pointed, and so on. Then cut out four of these shapes in fairly stiff card, two for each foot. To make a pair of well-fitting leather boots, construct them on the foot as far as

a
a and b. 1800–1830
c
c and d. 1830–1860
e
e and f. 1860–1890
g
g and h. 1890–1920
i
i and j. 1920–1960

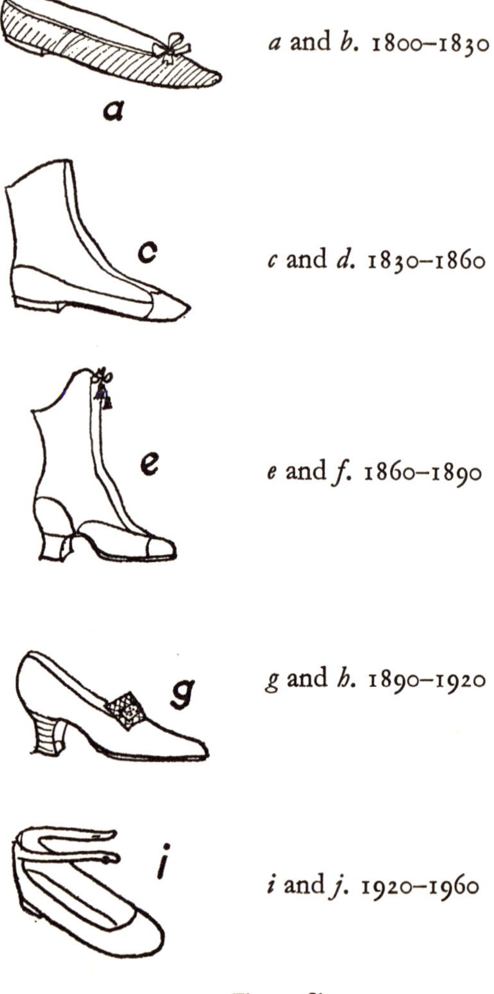

Fig. 44. Shoes

Slippers of satin, silk or kid, often stamped with a design and decorated with ribbons.

Boots made in satin or cashmere, often with patent-leather caps. Laced on the inside of the leg

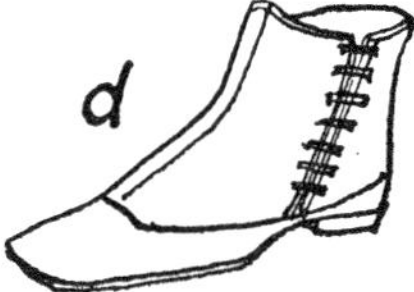

Boots in kid, calf or black leather with rounded toes. Shoes often with paste buckles or butterfly bows, and made in satin, or black and gold leather.

Black patent shoes with higher and more waisted heels. Children's boots are lower and are made in leather or white buckskin.

Ankle-strap slippers for children, in brown, black or patent leather. Sandals become almost standard wear for children.

Fig. 44. Shoes

tacking
grafting
glue
AND
machine
toecap
inner sole
outer sole
heel
Rosette

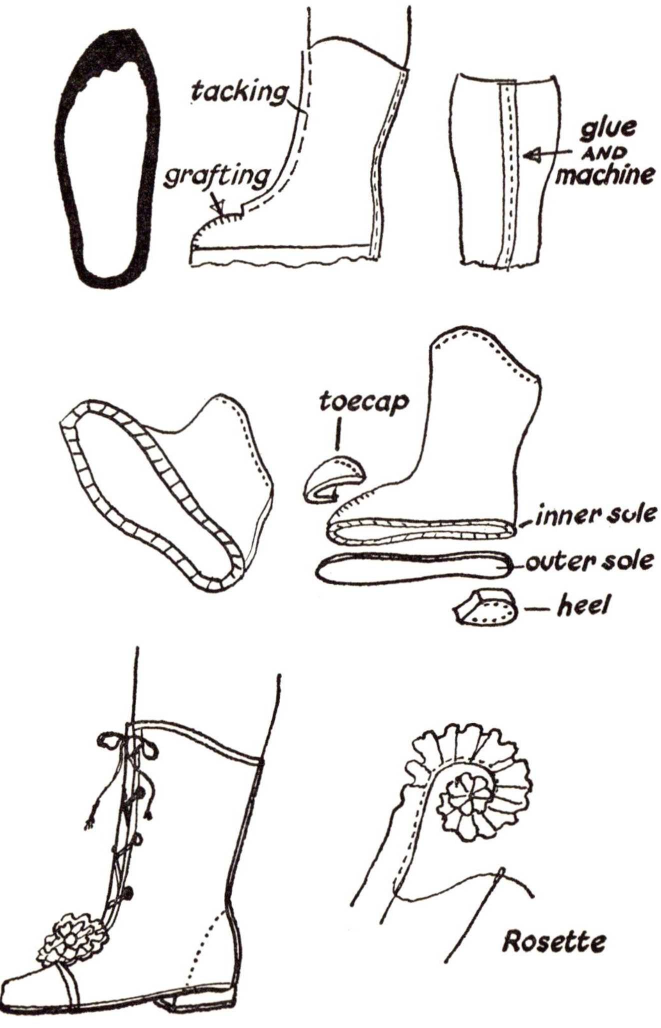

Fig. 45

practicable, stretching the leather tightly and cutting it to shape as you go. Cut the back seam so that it overlaps fractionally, glue with Copydex and then sew on the machine.

Butt joint the toe-piece and sew with tiny grafting stitches as far as the lacings. Now put a temporary tacking stitch from here to the top of the boot. Then turn the doll upside down and put a tiny blob of Copydex on the bottom of the doll's foot and stick the inner sole to this. (This is just to hold the inner sole temporarily in position and will wipe away quite cleanly afterwards.) Now cut the leather round the bottom edge, so that about $\frac{1}{8}''$ projects below the inner sole, snip it all round, apply Copydex and press on to the inner sole until it is all firmly in position. Whilst doing this you will, to some extent, be able to adjust the shape of the boot to take the form you envisage as most suitable for the period, particularly by easing the shape of the toe and if necessary padding with cotton wool.

Once these operations are complete, you will be able to undo the tacking stitches and slip the boot from its foot. A good finish will be achieved if you machine stitch a small turning all round the upper edge of the boot top.

Should you wish to make a toe-cap, then cut the appropriate piece of leather and put two rows of fine stitches along one edge, purely as decoration, and then snip, bend and glue the remaining edge as before, glueing the whole to the toe. Now comes the main sole, and to measure it, you draw round the boot as it now stands on to whatever material you plan to use. Although real leather would appear ideal for this purpose, I have found that, in practice, a most realistic effect can be achieved by using cork inner soles that have been worn until they are compressed and suitably discoloured.

A heel may be made of balsa wood, carved to shape, covered with leather and glued to the sole and itself heeled with the appropriate material.

Imitation nail heads can be made from the heads of dressmaker's pins, shortened and pressed into the heel.

If the boot is heeled, then there should be an arch to the foot and this you may effect by inserting between inner and outer soles a strip of thin, easily bent metal (Elastoplast tins are just the right gauge).

All that remains is to slip in the other two cardboard inner soles that were made at the beginning, and to make the eyelet holes and laces. The latter you may have amongst your store of possible materials, and I have found that Russian braid, which is made of two cords wrapped together in silk, will, with the cords removed, provide a suitable approximation to a silk bootlace. The ends can be finished off with strips of bent foil nipped into place.

Shoes can be made in the same way, except that you will be able to cut the top to shape whilst it is on the foot and it is not always necessary to have a join on the toes. Made in silk, satin or velvet, they become more difficult to handle because of the cloth's tendency to fray, so that it is a help to glue the cloth to a piece of stiffening right at the beginning and cut both at one time.

Some of the glues, such as Polycell, made for wallpapering, may come in handy at this point, for they do not stain the cloth if used sparingly.

When cutting out such shoes, leave a small turning around the top edges which can be glued down with Copydex.

To give an attractive finish to boots and shoes, you may well add some form of trimming, such as a small bow or a bead, an old button, a tassel or rosette, and the edges of the soles can be coloured to match the leather.

HATS

See Figs. 47–50 overleaf

In the main, hats are made of felt, straw, fur and woven materials and I will go on to describe how to make a fairly simple hat in each of these traditional materials and you will be able to adapt them for other styles.

Felt Hats

I had occasion recently to make a top hat for a wax doll, dressed in a velvet suit of about 1880, a child doll unsuitably clothed as a man. The original top hat had been lost. I used one of my own black fur felt hats because it was short haired and glossy. Before cutting into the felt I cut a pattern in thin

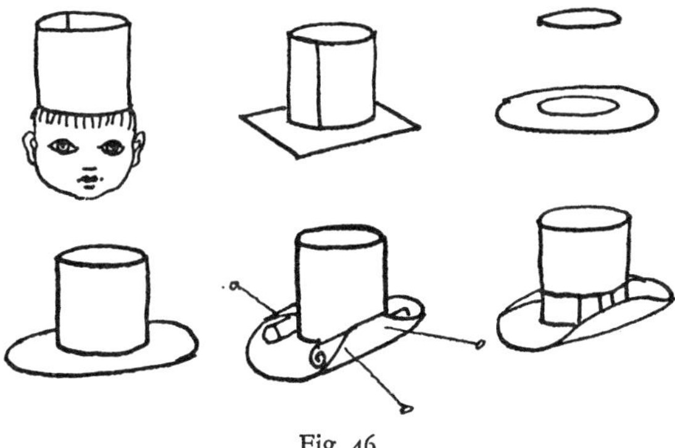

Fig. 46

card, holding it on to the head to gauge the right height and to find the circumference so that I could hold it on to another card and mark the round piece for the crown and the hole in the flat piece that was to form the brim.

I tried all these pieces on the head and adjusted them until I felt the shapes were correct. I was then able to cut out

Fig. 47

Fig. 48

Fig. 49

1950s

1960s

1960s

Fig. 50

the same shapes in felt and to sew them together with tiny grafting stitches. To get the curly brim of a real top hat I moistened the brim with a weak solution of Polycell and curled it round sausage shaped pieces of rag and left it pinned into position until it was dry and stiff. A ribbon tied in a flat bow finished it off.

Round or dome-shaped felt hats can be made over an improvised block, such as a stocking darner, a hard-boiled egg or a ball. Stretch the felt over the shape, steaming it,

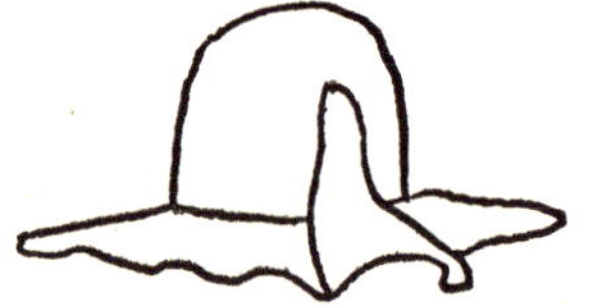

Fig. 51

and drawing the surplus to the back. The surplus is cut away and the seam joined with 'invisible' stitches. The brim can be eased and pressed into the shape you want and with such small felt hats there is seldom any need to wire the brim to hold the shape.

Straw Hats

The straw boater so often seen on dolls is a straightforward shape to make and has the added virtue of being suitable for wear by either sex. The woven straw can be bought in rolls of 6–8 yards and some is made up into four small strips sewn together, making a $\frac{1}{2}''$ wide strip.

Depending on the size of your doll you can, if you wish, split these strips down to single strands. As with the top hat, it is best to make a pattern of thin card so that you will finish up with a boater that fits. Take the strand of straw and, using a matching cotton, sew a running stitch along one edge of the strand and tighten this until the straw coils to form a circle.

Pin this with a drawing-pin through the cardboard pattern on to some firmer surface and continue to enlarge the straw crown of the hat, adding to the running stitches as you go and

Fig. 52

sewing the strands together with matching cotton. Now go down the sides of the hat and so on to form the brim, keeping it absolutely flat. If the straw is at all difficult to manage it may be damped and it should be steamed and pressed as you go along.

If you have an old straw hat to spare, then it will be easy to use this by, rather wastefully, taking the centre of the crown to make the top of the doll's boater.

Cloth Hats

Fig. 53 is a drawing of the hat of a doll about 125 years old. The cloth is pink cotton and the brim has five rows of cane to hold it into shape. The crown is supported by a circle of paper, cut, creased and pinched into the shape of a mob cap and covered by pink cotton. On the brim, the cotton is gathered on to five rows of cane, three of them to form the brim and two to form the headband. The rows of cane are separated from each other by running stitches that hold the gathered material into position. The crown is sewn to this and a band of cloth put inside for a headband. The hat is decorated with a strip of its own material, cut on the bias to make the edges roll inwards. A length of this is put round the hat and caught at intervals and a bow at the back has the same rolled edges.

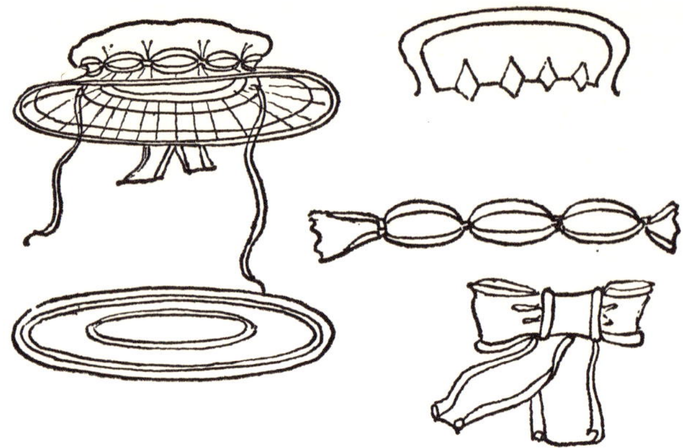

Fig. 53

Finally, from each side, strings of the same pink cotton fall so that they may be tied under the chin.

TRIMMINGS AND ACCESSORIES

Although important for the finished effect, trimmings should never be allowed to dominate the basic design: still less should they be expected to compensate for carelessly made clothes. It is not easy to choose the right trimming, and it is therefore best to try every kind against the garment and the doll. It is a help if you are able to do a few simple embroidery stitches and the better known trimmings.

Blanket Stitch and Cross Stitch

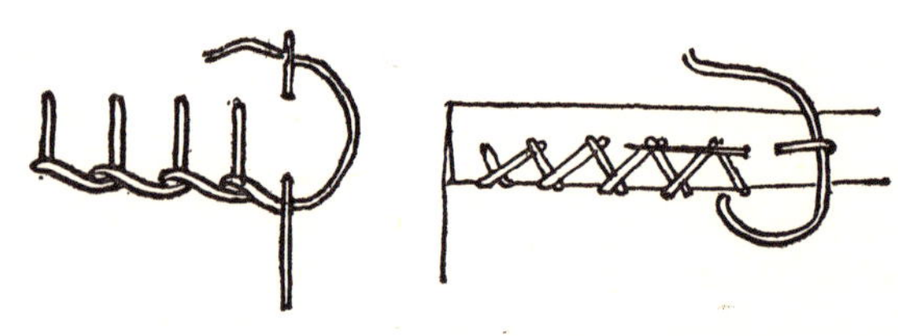

Figs. 54a and 54b

Used for the hems of flannel petticoats, these simple stitches are perhaps too well known for it to be necessary to describe their execution.

Chain Stitch

Fig. 54c

The thread is brought through at the top and held down with the left hand. The needle is pushed through where it last emerged, brought out again a short way on and pulled through, keeping the thread below the needle.

Faggoting

Faggoting is an embroidery stitch very popular with the Victorians and is used to join seams, to join on edgings and to insert lace.

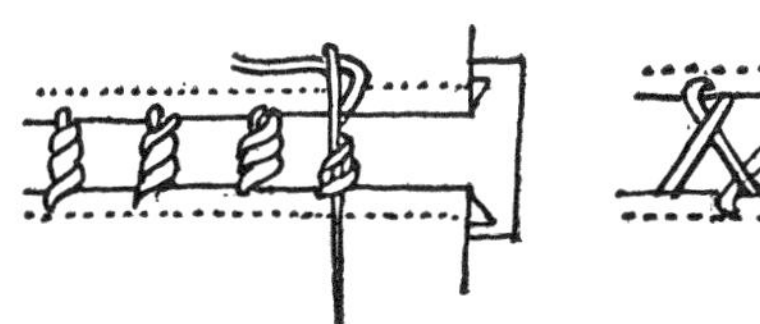

Fig. 55. Bar faggoting

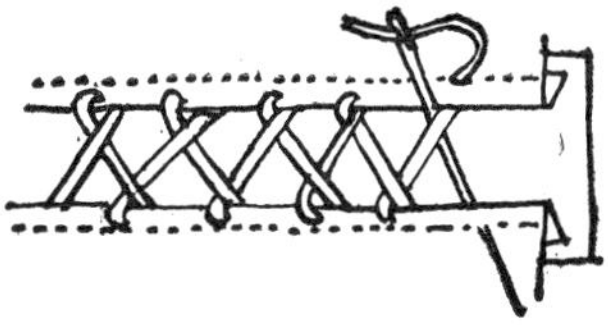

Fig. 56. Criss-cross faggoting

To prepare the material, take a strip of paper a little wider than the gap you need between the two pieces of material and tack the material to the paper, leaving the required gaps and having already turned back the edge of the fabric. There are two kinds of faggoting, bar and criss-cross faggoting. The bar faggoting is done by bringing the needle up from the underside of the material and close to the lower edge. The first stitch goes straight across the gap, and the needle is brought from the underside through the upper edge. The needle is twisted under and over the thread, and this forms the bar—repeated at regular intervals. For criss-cross faggoting the needle is brought through the lower edge of the cloth, taken diagonally across and upwards, then inserted from underneath on the top edge. This stitch is repeated alternately on the top and bottom pieces of cloth.

Feather Stitch

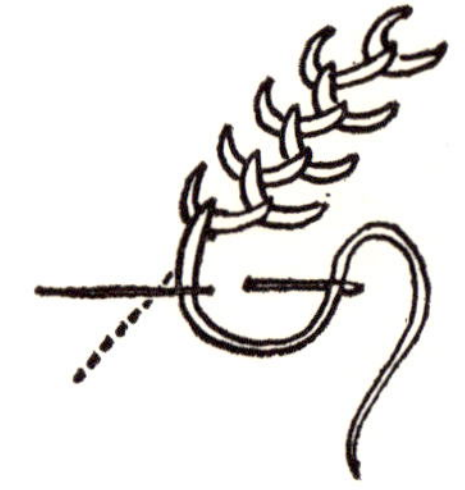

Fig. 57

The needle is brought through the material from the underside of the work, which is held in the left hand, and stuck in to the right and on the same level. It is then inserted a little to the left, on the same level and a stitch taken to the centre.

These two stitches are made alternately.

Shell Edging

Fig. 58

Usually too clumsy for dolls' clothes, it can occasionally look well if done with fine materials and one of its happier uses is for edging a hat.

You will have to turn a narrow hem on the material and, working from the wrong side of the material, insert the needle just below the hem, take two overcast stitches over the hem and pull them tight. Then slide the needle inside the hem for a short distance and bring the needle out again just below the hem and take two more overcast stitches. This is repeated with the stitches pulled as tight as possible.

Bows

If the bows are tied in the customary way from one or two lengths of material, then they will sit at awkward and exaggerated angles because of the small scale. It is therefore better to make them of separate pieces, folded and sewn into position.

Cockades

Fig. 59

These can be made of ribbon, working from left to right, with small pleats stitched to each other at the back to form a rosette, or half circle.

Ruching

This is done by taking a length of narrow ribbon, and stitching it down the centre on a sewing machine, pushing on both sides as you go. The effect is different from gathering by hand, for each tuck is pressed flat as it is sewn.

Lace

Lace trimmings should always be sewn on to the garments by hand with small stabbing stitches. New lace that looks too bold and white can be dipped in tea or coffee.

Pompoms

Those from bobble-edged fringe are especially useful for trimming shoes and, being usually of cotton, they will readily take a dye.

Feathers

Those from exotic birds and from budgerigars are of course excellent, but they can be reasonably well simulated by the small white feathers from poultry, dipped in ammonia, dyed a vivid colour and curled on a knife blade.

Jewellery

Woolworth's is the place—a rich source of dolls' jewellery. Earrings will make pendants, and small sections of earrings will break down for dolls' earrings.

Late Victorian and early Edwardian dolls of both sexes had their ears pierced and usually they wore very simple earrings of pale blue or pink beads.

From Woolworth's I have had a small gold cross, less than half an inch long, but it is well to remember not to exploit such lucky finds to excess or the effect will be cheapened.

Beads that have too small a hole for a needle to enter can be threaded with fine fuse-wire.

Both necklaces and earrings can be made from small decorative shells.

SECTION 3

Individual Dolls & their Clothing

IT IS MY intention now to take several real dolls that have passed through my hands and describe in detail their construction, dress, renovation and history, in so far as I am able, and to relate this to drawings, diagrams and patterns that might serve as a useful guide for the repair of dolls of similar times.

A Large Wax Doll of 1840 (Figs. 60 and 61)

This doll comes from the Harris Museum at Preston and was labelled '1840', a date that I felt to be confirmed by the style of dress, the pattern of the cloth, the eye mechanism and the turned-in toes.

It has a cotton body, filled with sawdust, and very long shapeless legs with the toes turned inwards in a way curiously characteristic of dolls about that time—and it is oddly similar in its proportions to the boudoir dolls of the 1920s.

The body has a centre back seam and darts at the sides to give it a waist. The forearms are of puce-coloured leather, with divided fingers and separate thumbs, and are only half as big as they would be on a real child of that size.

The head is made of composition, with a thin layer of wax, and has the typical half-smiling witless expression common to dolls of that time. The brown eyes, which have no pupils, can be made to open and close by pulling a wire that goes from the eyepiece through the body to emerge at the

Fig. 60. Wax Doll, 1840

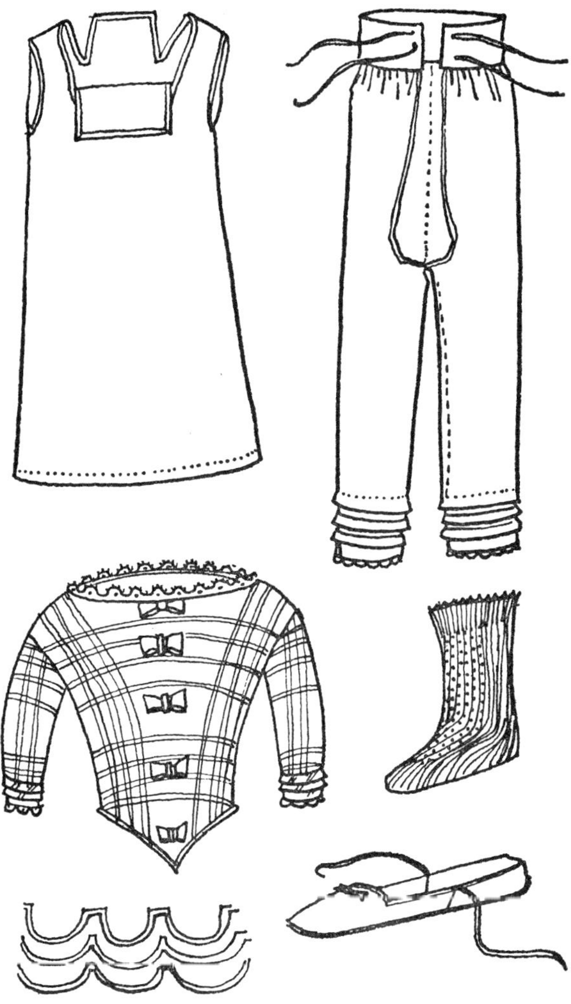

Fig. 61

waist. The head is topped with a separate circular crown of composition that has black ringlets glued to it.

She wears long, narrow, untrimmed trousers that are tucked at the bottom, a chemise of untrimmed white cotton with flaps at the neck and a rather elaborate petticoat of ripple-weave wool, scalloped round the bottom band, trimmed with scarlet wool braid and tied at the back with tapes.

The dress is a beautiful dark plaid silk, red, green and blue, with a narrow white check, and it is lined with cotton, the whole wonderfully sewn and in perfect condition. It is edged with silk lace and trimmed with bows of the same plaid.

The back opening fastens with crude brass hooks (newly invented) and the dress is made to fit very tightly, both in the bodice and the sleeves, which have three tucks at the bottom and are inserted low, off the shoulders, as was then the mode.

I have described the fine hat worn by this doll in the previous chapter, for it is one of the most attractive I have encountered.

She wears white openwork socks, but the shoes are missing. The kind of shoe to make would be the ballet-slipper type with a a slightly square toe, of black or white satin: or an elastic boot of satin or cashmere with black kid toe-caps decorated with bows.

The common dress materials of this era were muslin, linen, gingham, foulards, merino, cashmere and printed chintz, and mixtures of silk and wool. Checks and stylised floral patterns were very popular, but the more rich and elaborate velvets, satins and flowered silks that were worn by older women on formal occasions are not very suitable for dolls, magnificent and tempting as they are. The Chiné silk, of muted colour, fashionable by 1840, would be an ideal material to use for a doll. Aprons, often of frilled satin, were worn at this time, with or without a bib, and shawls of all kinds were very fashionable. Muffs, smaller than those of previous years, were of fur, satin or swansdown.

Long earrings and short necklaces were worn and bunches of artificial flowers were often carried. Brooches were worn and watches hung from the waist and, not surprisingly, the older the women, the more bedecked with jewellery.

A Small Wax Doll of 1850 (Figs. 62 and 63)

This pretty doll is made of poured wax so that head, arms and legs are all hollow. It is 18″ high and was made in England about 1850. The blown glass eyes are a deep, unreal ultramarine and are fixed into the wax head. The ash-blonde hair is of poor quality at the back, whilst better hair is set into slits at the front of the wax head. On the top of the head two rows of slits interlace each other. The locks of back hair are set to grow back and the fringe forward.

The shoulders were broken into several pieces. I tried to mend them by sticking the pieces together with animal glue, which is the only glue that will adhere to wax, but without much success, and the wax was too thin to allow of adhesion by melting. In desperation I glued the broken pieces on to the cloth body. Over them I stretched and glued, with Copydex, a single piece of fine gauze that held them all together. To disguise these fractures and to support the whole I added strips of old lace which came right over the shoulders and on to the body, glued again with Copydex. A band of lace went round the cloth chest to cover the ends, and a necklace of minute beads hid the join at the neck.

The body is made of cotton, stuffed with hair, probably cow hair, and the body and legs to the knee joint are made in one piece with lines of stitching at the hips and knees to allow for bending. The wax head, forearms and lower half of the legs are sewn on to the body through small holes made in the wax.

The dress is of white spotted muslin, trimmed with fine cotton lace and ruched Prussian blue silk with pinked edges.

Fig. 62. Wax Doll, 1850

Fig. 63

In the 1850's, muslins with raised embroidery were fashionable for children's clothes. It is made of two pieces, the top lined, and fastened at the front with large brass hooks, the skirt gathered on to a band, buttoned at the back of the waist and trimmed with lace. It is mid-calf length as for a young child. Other children and adults wore long skirts.

The white cotton chemise is trimmed at the neck and sleeves with narrow lace, and the waist-length petticoat is tucked and decorated with a twisted cord embroidery and fastened at the back with a home-made linen button.

The long pantaloons cover the ankles and, as they are intended to be seen and admired, they are elaborately decorated. Some pantaloons of this period have separate legs that tie below the knee so that they can be even more elaborate and always clean. On this doll they are tucked at the hips, helping to hold out the skirts, as well as on the legs, and have both lace insertions and edgings. They are open, back and front, to about the middle of the thigh and they fasten at the back of the waist with a linen button. The sewing machine had not been invented at this time, so all had been sewn by hand.

The doll wears a beautiful straw hat, of rather oriental style, lined with pink silk, the crown and the edge of the brim decorated with pink silk velvet ribbon: and hanging from the back is a large bow of pink corded ribbon. She wears white cotton socks and slippers of bronze kid with rosettes of brown satin.

Had this doll been supplied with a larger wardrobe, it might have included a paletot, which was an overcoat for girls and boys. Such characteristic garments were often of grey cloth, three-quarter length, and trimmed with braid.

Bonnets were worn by girls and were miniature versions of the adult, face hiding, fashion. They were lined with gathered silk and trimmed with ribbon, flowers, or a single feather lying along the top of the brim.

Boys would probably wear straw hats lined and trimmed with silk and ribbon. This particular doll has a fringe and a headband, but a centre parting would be more typical of the period, with a smooth head and ringlets falling to the shoulders or looped up in plaits.

A Boy Doll of 1880 (Figs. 64 and 65)

This is an Armand Marseille doll, made in Germany about 1890, but I have chosen to dress it in the costume of the early 1880's, a not unusual occurrence that may be accounted for (in other cases) by a mother's choice of clothes of her own hey-day when she dressed a doll for a child.

When it came to me, this doll was in desperate straits, so that almost everything had to be made or repaired. The china head was broken, fortunately across the forehead where it could be hidden by a fringe. The wig was beyond repair so I made a new one with real hair with a central knot (see page 35), and because I had so little hair, I decided to dress it as a boy, whose short haircut would be more acceptable.

The long, thin body stuffed with wood-wool and made of very poor pink cotton had two black cotton stumps for legs and no arms. I replaced the cotton stumps with papier-mâché legs and made new hands and arms of the same material.

In the 1880's, plush and velvet were worn a great deal by children as well as adults, and, because it was so typical of this period, I decided to make a boy's velvet suit, in spite of all I have said earlier in this book about the unsuitability of such heavy materials, but I had an old piece of deep blue velvet and decided that, if I did not use any gathers, I might manage it.

I have drawn the patterns that I made on the doll for the suit. The jacket has a front fastening piped with bright red and with tiny pearl buttons. The cuffs and trousers are similarly piped with red and the separate skirt is pleated in large folds on to a waistband.

Fig. 64. Boy Doll, 1880s

TROUSER PATTERN
JACKET BACK
JACKET FRONT
SHIRT
CUFF
JACKET SLEEVE

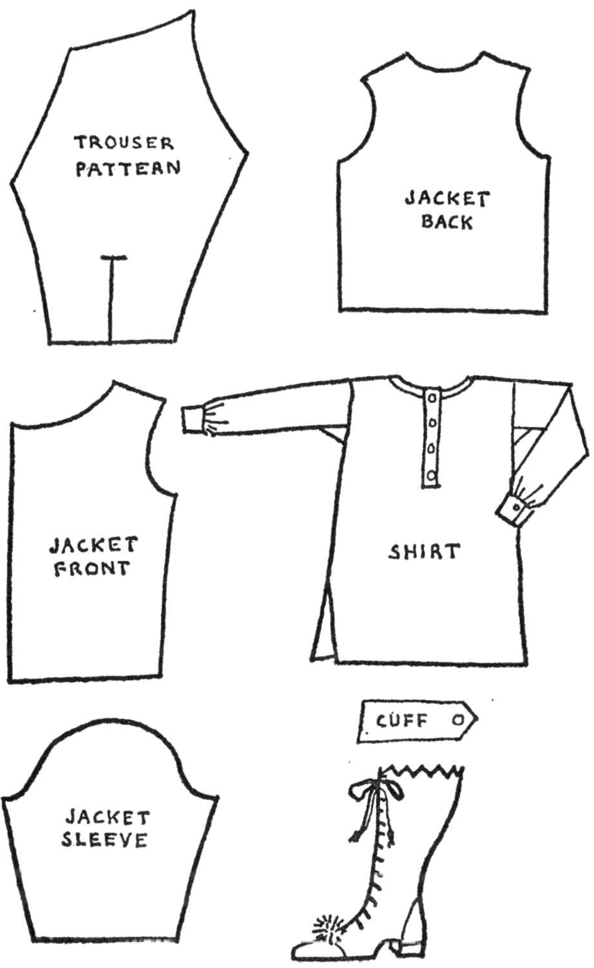

Fig. 65

The collar is an old lace collar cut down and the spare bits used for hanging cuffs, with a red bow at the neck. The waist has a large dark blue sash, tied at the back in a large bow. He wears grey ribbed woollen stockings, then very fashionable, having just replaced the cotton ones of preceding years. The boots have front fastenings and tassels.

The large straw hat (see page 85) has a red band and streamers. I had no old red ribbon and the new looked too bright, so I chose a red cotton paris binding.

His underclothes would be a shirt and drawers, cotton for summer, flannel in winter.

Twins of the mid-1880s (*Figs 66 and 67*)

Baby dolls or child dolls, as distinct from the adult figures of earlier and recent times, have been made since the middle of the 18th century and many of them are of wax, and occasionally you come across them in pairs, dressed as twins.

The particular twins I illustrate are 20″ high, with wax heads and shoulders and arms and legs of composition. It is their legs with black boots, white stockings and red garters that suggest the 1880s.

They have blue eyes and fair hair that is rather sparingly arranged across the front of their heads. The bonnets hide their baldness. They are most beautifully clad in layers of fine cotton underclothes, all sewn by hand, and they have dresses of fine woollen cashmere, one a faded pink, the other a very faded blue. The dresses, though not identical, are very alike, with high waists, gathered bodices, tucked sleeves and frilled hemlines. They have sashes, and bows on their sleeves and bonnets, all to match their pinks and blues.

Fig. 66. Wax Doll, mid-1880s

Fig. 67

A Bisque Doll of the 1890s (Figs. 68 to 71)

The doll has a jointed kid body and it is dressed in the most beautiful and elaborate way imaginable. There is a cotton chemise and under-petticoat, cotton drawers trimmed with fine cotton lace, a cream flannel petticoat decorated with cream silk buttonholing and floral motifs, and a cotton petticoat trimmed with hand-made cotton lace.

The dress is a pale blue cashmere, with a tucked bodice and pleated skirt and with blue feather stitching round the hemline. The very full sleeves are in three tiers, the bottom edge trimmed with fine lace. The splendid pinafore is trimmed with broderie anglaise.

Her coat and bonnet are of white cotton pique, trimmed with cream imitation fur, and over the coat there is an extra cape similarly trimmed and tied with a silk ribbon. She wears white cotton knee length socks and brown kid ankle-strap shoes. If indeed a child of that time wore so many clothes they must have been a considerable burden.

Fig. 68. Bisque Doll of the 1890s

Fig. 69

Fig. 70

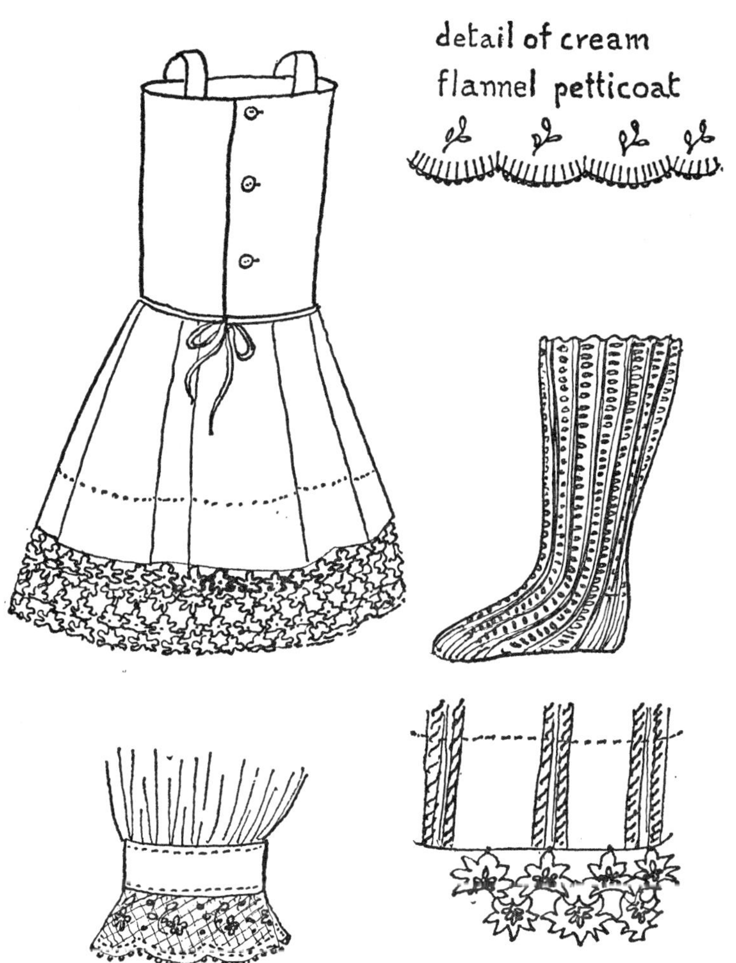

Fig. 71

A Bisque Doll of 1910 (Figs. 72 to 74)

This two-foot tall doll bears on the back of its neck the mark 'A.M. Made in Germany', which tells us that it was made by the firm of Armand Marseille of that country and that it was made at some time after 1890, for, from that time, all dolls imported into England had to be marked with their country of origin. The doll was obviously made before the First World War and, by the style and feel of it, I would imagine it to have been made about 1910.

The very pretty bisque head has deep blue sleeping eyes and long, thick lashes and the well-modelled body of turned wood and composition is ball-jointed. At the end of the last century and at the beginning of this, Armand Marseille dolls were exceptionally popular and therefore plentiful. The heads and shoulders are of bisque, but the bodies of the earlier ones are of cloth and kid, and the later ones, like this example, have swivel necks and jointed bodies. Usually the wigs were made of a fringe of hair stitched to a canvas cap, but this wig was missing so I made one of real hair, black and curly.

When I bought her, all the clothes were missing, so I have had to make the complete set. The underclothes include a short-sleeved vest of machine knitted silk and wool rib, tied at the neck with a silk drawstring, fine woollen combinations bound down the centre opening with narrow white tape and fastened with small white pearl buttons, and a liberty bodice strengthened with white tape that extends below the bottom edge at front and sides to provide a buttonhole for stockings. All the edges of this garment are bound with white tape, and it buttons down the front. These underclothes I made from a baby's old and worn vest, using the ribbed edges for the ends of sleeves and legs. I have illustrated a different kind of stays worn a little earlier and at this time. They were of red or white quilted flannel and were wrapped around the body, one end threaded through a slot in the garment and tied to the other end at the front of the waist. They had adjustable shoulder straps, and tapes to support stockings.

The white cotton knickers have a frill round the legs and reach to the top of the kneecap. They are partly open at the sides so that they can button to the stays (the front first) and form a flap at the back.

Such white cotton knickers were worn with almost all clothes, except navy-blue sailor suits and school uniforms, which called for the use of navy blue serge or flannel knickers of slightly different construction. For these, the body band was sewn to the front of the garment and buttoned at the back of the waist: and instead of a frill at the knees, they were gathered into a band and buttoned.

With this century, the gymnasium and games field were an accepted part of the schoolgirl's life; clothes were rather more practical and petticoats were no longer worn with uniform. Nevertheless, petticoats continued to be worn by a great many children and they were usually of cotton or flannel, plain for everyday clothes and elaborate for party dresses. They usually had a sleeveless bodice with a high, round neck, buttoned down the front or back and tied at the waist with a drawstring. The skirt was gathered on to the bodice, although it was less full than before, and often had tucks and edgings of lace or crochet work.

During this hey-day of Imperial Fleets, all the children of Europe seemed to wear sailor suits and so I inevitably chose to dress this doll in the characteristic white flannel sailor suit, with a knee-length pleated skirt buttoned at the waist. The blouse has a band, buttoning either side of the waist, long sleeves, a navy-blue sailor collar with rows of white braid round the edge, a striped navy-and-white modesty vest and a black satin neckerchief.

Fig. 72. Bisque Doll, 1910

Fig. 73

Fig. 74

On the breast pocket I have embroidered an anchor, and the wrist bands I have edged with navy-blue Russian braid. The sailor hat of straw I made in the way described in the earlier chapter on hats, and, as the only straw I had available was too new looking, I put it out in the sun for several days and it quickly weathered (but without allowing it to get damp because of warping).

The doll wears long black stockings and the boots described on page 76. Doll's shoes sold in the Edwardian toyshops were almost all of the flat-soled ankle-strapped kind, tied or buttoned on the insteps. About this time, children wore black or brown stockings for every day and white on Sunday, and only young children wore socks.

Reefer coats and man-o'-war hats were fashionable and also hats with flat crowns and wide brims, made of white cotton and trimmed with broderie anglaise. For children, long, loose, curly hair was much admired and curl rags were put in every night. Generous bows of satin ribbon, worn at one side of the face or at the nape of the neck, held this luxuriant hair away from the face.

Poupard Doll (*Fig. 75*)

These dolls are primarily musical toys or rattles.

Above the waist they are the same as all other dolls, but under their skirts they hide either a rattle, a whistle or a simple musical box.

Their French name—'baby doll'—would imply that they are intended for babies to play with, although their elaborate construction seems rather unsuitable for such a perilous role. Not only are they the most decorative of toys, but they provide an ideal opportunity to use up a spare head, and this is what I have done with the Armand Marseille head shown here.

First I had a wooden handle turned on a lathe, and this goes right through the doll and is fixed firmly into the head with

Fig. 75. Poupard

plaster of Paris. The stuffed calico body goes down to the waist, where it is tied to the handle and over a tin containing pebbles, which forms both hips and rattle. I dressed her in rich dark green velvet, with old satin dyed to a brilliant green as an overdress. This I trimmed with rather tarnished gold and silver lace and braid, golden glass beads and rosettes of green ribbon. From the waist I hung transparent ribbons that ended with bells. The rattle beneath is hidden by a petticoat of gauzy frills.

Pedlar Dolls (Fig. 76)

These repositories for trinkets were most popular in the 18th and early 19th centuries and their miniature stock-in-trade could be bought in all the toy shops and fairs and presumably from the pedlars themselves.

The dolls are mainly old women dolls, with an occasional old man, and are usually made of carved wood, on a stand rather than legs. A limited number of wax pedlars were made at the beginning of the 19th century. Rather a lot of pedlar dolls have survived, presumably because they were treated as ornaments, or collections, rather than as toys: indeed, in some cases, they lived under glass domes, like artificial flowers and birds. Their clothes frequently follow a rather dull tradition of a dress with a quilted skirt, a white pinafore and a red cape and bonnet.

These pedlars can play a most useful role for the doll collector, where their trays provide a display for all the miniature objects that have accumulated over the years, and when the pedlar has been loaded to excess the collector can make a miniature trunk to hold the surplus.

The pedlar doll that I have drawn is one that I made for myself after being shown how to do it by the American doll maker and collector, Lewis Sorenson, and, although this may not be strictly within the scope of this book, I feel that a

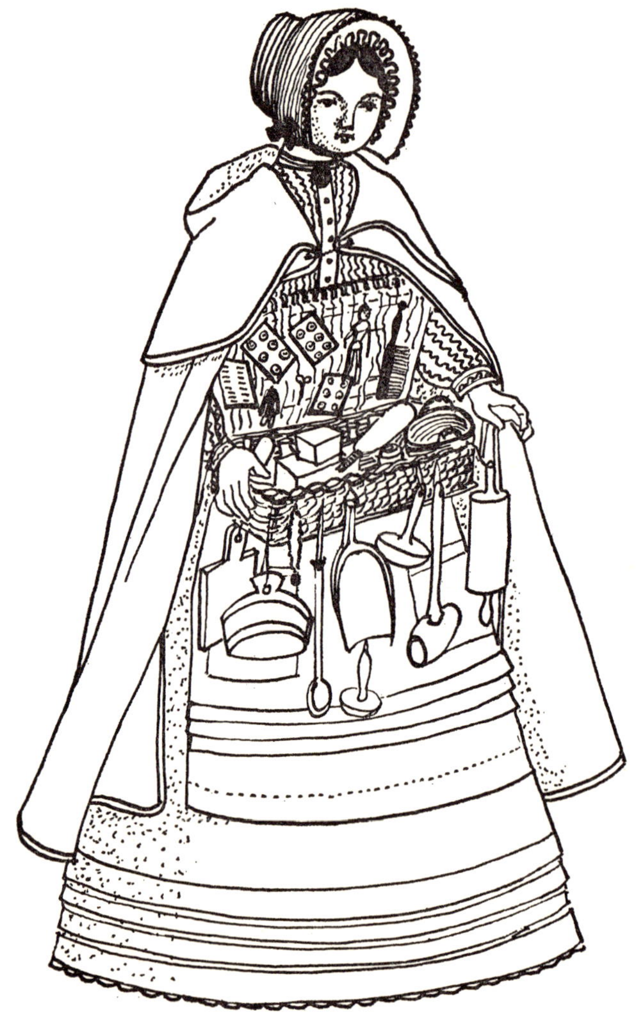

Fig. 76. Pedlar

description of the construction of such a pedlar doll might be of sufficient use or interest to the doll collector to justify its inclusion.

I bought one of the crudely carved wooden heads that are still available in England, although they must be thirty years old, and used it as a base, on to which I modelled with Plastone new features appropriate to a pedlar, and from the same material I modelled a pair of hands, coloured all of these with tempera and dipped them in wax, as described earlier in the book. Because of the bonnet, only a wisp of hair will show and a proper wig is unnecessary, so I glued grey locks around the forehead. The body I made of strong calico, stuffed very stiff and hard, which it would need to be for its particular role. A good stuffing for this purpose is newspaper or the bits of cork used for packing grapes. A stick up the centre will help support the body and its eventual load. The head and shoulders are glued into position.

In order to support the whole figure firmly, I made a cone-shaped stand of stiff card, fitted round the waist and glued to a circular cardboard base. The hands and forearms of modelled Plastone were then attached to the loosely filled calico upper arms sewn to the shoulders, and the pedlar was ready for dressing.

I first covered the base of the stand with felt that I turned up the sides of the figure for $\frac{1}{2}''$ and glued into position. Next I made a petticoat out of an old piece of broderie anglaise, gathered and stitched to the waist and loosely stitched round the bottom edge of the felt base.

A blouse was made of some old cotton that had a dark background printed with a very small floral pattern. This I made with a high neckline and a fitted bodice. I was able to adjust the shape of the figure with cottonwool padding, to form a bosom, because the doll was essentially a fixed figure, never to be undressed. An old earring made a brooch for the neckband, and small white beads were the buttons. Long sleeves with cuffs were fastened with the same little beads. The skirt I made of the same cotton, lined with a stiff material, quilted and gathered to form a bell-shaped skirt. The apron, of white cotton with three tucks and two pockets, was very stiffly starched before it was tied on to the doll.

From my collection of scraps, I took a piece of fine old red cashmere to use for the cape. I was able to measure its length on the doll, cut it out in one piece and bind right round it with black cotton bias binding. This cape folds over at the neck to form a long collar, fastened on the chest with two small brass buttons and a short length of gold chain. I made a mob cap out of white muslin, well starched and frilled round the edges, and this I arranged on the head so that it fitted well over the ears. On top of this goes the straw bonnet made of narrow lengths of plaited straw stitched together to form the correct shape.

I bought a small basket in one of the many gift shops in our village. It is just a few inches long and has a hinged lid, but as it looked too new and bright, I gave it a coat of old brown varnish. A tape held the lid open and hung the basket from the pedlar's neck

The collection of miniature wooden kitchen utensils, which I hung on to the outside of the basket, were made in Yugoslavia, beautifully turned and finished and in scale to a 20″ pedlar doll. I have made several such pedlars, to carry different wares, and for one that I dressed in a blue print dress I made a basketful of bread. This bread I made of equal quantities of salt and flour, mixed with a little water and baked for a long time in a very slow oven so that it became rock hard. I made it in all sizes and shapes, cottage loaves, cobs, plaits, rolls and a long French roll to go under the doll's arm.

I made another pedlar doll, using a wax head that Lewis Sorenson had made and given to me, and his tray I filled with

Fig. 77. Bride, 1880s

miniature toys, some of my own making and some bought. There is a small dolls' house, cricket bats, kites, tops and whips, dolls, paper parasols, wooden soldiers and horses and so on.

With a male pedlar, there is the awful problem of supporting the figure and its ill-balanced tray on two thin legs, which calls for a stand. His boots were perhaps the greatest challenge.

A Bride (*Fig. 77*)

There are a lot of old dolls dressed as brides and it may be reasonable to suppose that some are intended as portraits—replicas of some actual wedding-dress. The present fashion for teenage dolls, and their manufacture to that adult scale, makes it now much easier for people to dress dolls as grown-ups: and what better than to copy the important, elaborate and expensive wedding-dress that will be far too bulky and useless to keep.

More often than not, the actual cloth will be too thick to put on a doll, but some thinner material that resembles it can usually be found. The trimmings and bouquet could be of very narrow ribbon, those miniature artificial flowers that are sold to decorate wedding cakes appropriately enough would make the bouquet, and very fine transparent gauze the veil.

SECTION 4

CONSERVATION

ONCE ALL THE dolls are restored, re-dressed and clean, it would be heartbreaking were they to receive further damage. Yet their storage presents peculiar and difficult problems, for the older they get, the more fragile they become. Even one doll is a difficult object to display and the majority of collectors soon find themselves storing their dolls in old suitcases and under beds. In spite of the attraction of glazed cabinets and special filing cabinets, the suitcase is particularly well suited for this job. Most collectors of dolls show their collection at exhibitions, away from home, and suitcases full of dolls, stacked ready and labelled, are probably by far the most convenient form of storage. I have also found a gentleman's wardrobe, with sliding shelves tailor-made for the purpose.

Before it is put away, each doll should be labelled and carefully examined and treated with a little D.D.T. powder to discourage moths. The wigs are particularly dangerous areas for such development and I have seen a Jumeau doll with a cork dome full of grubs after some years of storage. Wooden dolls are, of course, subject to attack by woodworm and any small holes should be injected wtih Rentokil or some similar preventative. The arms and legs can be protected by cardboard rolls or cottonwool and the dolls packed with crumpled paper. If you put your dolls into plastic bags, you must ensure that there are sufficient holes or they may suffer from condensation, particularly the wax heads, and such damp will easily form mildew on clothes.

Dolls with sleeping eyes should be packed face down so that the eyes remain open.

When dolls are wanted for an exhibition is the usual time for smartening them up. Clothes can be washed and improvements effected, such as a new pair of shoes, or a hat that has been envisaged but not made whilst the doll was out of sight. Should such accessories look too fresh for the rest of the doll, be drastic and expose the offending article to bright sunlight. It will soon fade and age to match its surroundings.

The ideal way to display dolls, when money is no object, is for each of them to have properly made stands, but such luxury is rarely available and most of us are obliged to improvise. Dolls with long, full skirts are the simplest to manage, for their legs can be put into an ornament or a tumbler. Others will have to recline on a sloping surface.

Dolls should not be exposed for very long to direct light or they will fade, especially the wax and plastic dolls, and particularly the clothes. Strong sunlight will also make the clothes and hair brittle and liable to rot and break.

Should you wish to make a copy of a doll mark, so that you can identify it, the simplest way to do this is to lay a piece of thin paper over the mark and rub a soft pencil or wax crayon across it. The mark will show up in white, like a brass rubbing. To photograph such a mark, it may be strengthened by sprinkling with some dark powder which will stay in the grooves and dust off the ridges.

A great many museums have collections of dolls and toys and, although I cannot hope to provide a complete list, here are some of the better known collections.

Some Museums in which Dolls can be seen in Britain

Abbey House Museum, Kirkstall, Leeds
Ashmolean Museum, Oxford
Barry Elder Doll Museum, Carr House, Southport
Bethnal Green Museum, Cambridge Heath Road, London, E.2

Bolling Hall Museum, Bradford 4, Yorks.
Bramber Museum, Bramber, Nr. Steyning, Sussex (Not dolls, but animal tableaux of the Victorian era)
Bowes Museum, Barnard Castle, Co. Durham (Good dolls' houses as well)
Beatrix Potter's House, Sawrey, Nr. Ambleside (Only two dolls, but also the dolls' house made famous by the book 'Tale of Two Bad Mice')
Bristol Folk Museum
Cambridge and County Folk Museum
Chester Museum
Claverton Manor, Bath (The American museum in Britain. Miniature houses and shops)
Cliff Castle Museum, Keighley, Nr. Bradford
Derby Museum, Wardwick, Derby
Doll Museum, Oken's House, Castle Street, Warwick
Fitzwilliam Museum, Cambridge
Geffrye Museum, Shoreditch, London
Gunnersbury Park Museum, London
Harris Museum, Preston (Some new additions)
Hereford City Museum, Broad Street, Hereford
Holland House, London
Hollytrees Museum, Colchester
Hove Museum
Horniman Museum, Dulwich
Hull Museum
Lanhydrock House, Bodmin, Cornwall
London Museum
Luton Museum
Museum of Childhood and Costume, Blithfield Hall, Nr. Rugeley
Museum of Childhood, Edinburgh
Nottingham City Museum, The Castle, Nottingham
Pitt Rivers Museum, Oxford
Pitt Rivers Museum, Farnham Royal, Dorset

Pollock's Toy Museum, London
Priest's House, West Hoathly
Queen's Park Art Gallery, Harpurhey, Manchester
Red House, Christchurch, Hants.
The Rotunda, Oxford (Dolls' houses)
Royal Pumproom Museum, Harrogate
Royal Scottish Museum, Edinburgh
Salisbury Museum
St. Albans Museum
Saltwell Park Museum, Gateshead
Shibden Hall, Halifax
Snowhill Manor, Gloucestershire
Somerset County Museum, Taunton
The Stroud Museum, Lansdown, Gloucestershire
Tollcross Museum, Glasgow
Toy Museum, Rottingdean, Nr. Brighton
Tunbridge Wells Museum
Victoria & Albert Museum, London
Warwick County Museum, Market Place, Warwick
Wellcome Museum, London
Welsh Folk Museum, St. Fagan's Castle, Cardiff
Willis Museum, Basingstoke, Hants.
Windsor Castle, Windsor (Queen's dolls' house also on view).
Woburn Abbey
Worthing Museum
York Castle Museum

Some Museums in which dolls can be seen in the U.S.A.

California: Los Angeles, Annex to home of Mrs. George Butler Griffin, 2,500 dolls. Santa Monica, Hawkins' Doll Hospital and Museum.

Connecticut: Hartford, Children's Museum—Antique and Foreign

District of Columbia: The National Museum; Department of the Interior; Indian Dolls (shop).

Florida: Inverness, Famous People in Miniature, Route 41, Highway.

Illinois: Chicago, Historical Society.

Indiana: Greenfield, James Whitcomb Riley Old Home Society. Indianapolis; Children's Museum.

Iowa: Cedar Rapids, Howe's Doll House, the Doll-A-Rama, Route 1.

Kansas: Topeka, Kansas State Historical Museum.

Maine: Portland, Maine Historical Society.

Maryland: Baltimore, Enoch Pratt Free Library.

Massachusetts: Boston, The Harrison Gray Otis House; The Children's Museum. Salem, Essex Institute. Worcester, Dolls' Paradise Museum.

Michigan: Dearborn, Henry Ford Museum. Detroit, Children's Museum.

New Hampshire: West Chesterfield, Museum of Old Dolls and Toys.

New York: Bergen, Maretta's Doll and Toyland Museum. Brooklyn, Children's Museum. New York City, Traphagen School of Design, Metropolitan Museum of Art.

Ohio: Cleveland, Cleveland Museum of Art.

Oregon: Wecoma Beach, Lacey's Doll House Museum.

Pennsylvania: Philadelphia, Franklin Institute.

Vermont: Brattleboro, Route 9. Museum of Marie McCollum. Shelburne, Shelburne Museum's Collection of Dolls and Doll Houses. Waterbury, House of a Thousand Dolls.

Virginia: Richmond, Virginia Historical Society.

Washington: Lake Stevens, East of Everett Frontier Village Museum.

Wisconsin: Milwaukee, Public Library.

For a more complete list of Doll Museums, see *Dolls: A New Guide for Collectors,* by Clara Hallard Fawcett, Branford, Newton, Mass., 1965.

American equivalents, or descriptions, of British proprietary products

RENTOKIL A woodworm killer readily available in the U.S. from: Crafts Shops Department, Colonial Williamsburg Inc., Williamsburg, Virginia.

POLYFILLA AND POLYCELL are not available in the U.S., but there are many American equivalents. Polyfilla is a type of plaster; dental plaster could be used in its place. Polycell is a plastic adhesive used for hanging wallpaper.

ROWNEY'S EGG TEMPERA COLOURS are available throughout the U.S. and are made by no other manufacturers.

ROWNEY'S CRYLA COLOURS can be bought in the U.S. They are acrylic resin colours.

VINATEX This product is not normally obtainable in America, but can be bought direct from Alex Tiranti Ltd., 72 Charlotte Street, London W.1. It is a vinyl resin, hot melt compound.

COPYDEX Available throughout the U.S.

SELLOTAPE is sold in the U.S. 'Scotch' tape is a similar product.

PLASTICINE Available in the U.S.

PLASTONE Not normally available in the U.S. A self-hardening modelling material sold as suitable for decorating wood, china, glass with relief decoration and also for making full relief models in the round.

GESSO POWDER made by C. Roberson & Co. Ltd., 71 Parkway, London, N.W.1 is not normally available in the U.S. It is a finely ground powder that can be mixed with water to a creamy consistency, drying relatively hard with adhesion to the surface to which it is applied.